ESTRENO CONTEMPORARY SPANISH PLAYS

General Editors

Iride Lamartina-Lens and Susan Berardini
Modern Languages Dept.
Pace University, New York, NY

Advisory Board

Sharon Carnicke
Professor of Theatre and
Associate Dean
University of Southern California

Sandra Harper
Editor, *Estreno*
Ohio Wesleyan University

Marion Peter Holt
Critic and Translator
New York City

Steven Hunt
Director and Theatre Professor
Iowa City

Felicia Hardison Londré
Curators' Professor of Theatre
University of Missouri – Kansas City
American Theatre Fellow

Grant McKernie
Professor of Theatre
University of Oregon

Anjali Vashi
Professor of Theatre
Pace University

Phyllis Zatlin
Professor of Spanish
Rutgers, The State University

ESTRENO Collection of Contemporary Spanish Plays

General Editors: Iride Lamartina-Lens and Susan Berardini

GONE ASTRAY

ITZIAR PASCUAL

GONE ASTRAY:

CASTAWAYS
(*Varadas*)

HOLIDAY OUT
(*Holliday Aut*)

MEOWLESS
(*Miauless*)

Translated from the Spanish
by
Phyllis Zatlin

ESTRENO Plays
New York, New York
2006

ESTRENO Contemporary Spanish Plays 29
General Editors: Iride Lamartina-Lens and Susan Berardini
Modern Languages Dept.–PNY
Pace University
41 Park Row
New York, NY 10038 USA

Library of Congress Cataloging in Publication Data
Pascual, Itziar, 1967-
  Gone Astray
  Bibliography:
  Contents: Castaways. Holiday Out. Meowless.
  1. Pascual, Itziar, 1967-
      Translation, English.
  I. Zatlin, Phyllis. II. Title.
1Library of Congress Control No.: 20069267
ISBN: 1-888463-24-4 / 978-1-888463-24-8

© 2006 Copyright by ESTRENO
Original plays © Itziar Pascual: Varadas, 2002. Holliday Aut, 1996. Miauless, 2000.
Translation © Phyllis Zatlin, 2002, 2006.

All rights reserved.
No part of this publication may be reproduced or transmitted in any form or by any means, electronic or mechanical, including photocopy, recording, or any information storage or retrieval system now known or to be invented, without permission in writing from the publishers, except by a reviewer who wishes to quote brief passages in connection with a review written for inclusion in a magazine, newspaper, or broadcast.

Published with support from
Office of the Provost
Pace University
and
Program for Cultural Cooperation
Between Spain's Ministry of Education, Culture and Sports and
United States Universities

Cover: Jeffrey Eads

TABLE OF CONTENTS

About the Playwright, by Susan Berardini ………………………..	viii
Director's Note on *Holiday Out*, by Michael Schlick …………..	xv
A Note on the Plays, by Jennifer Zachman ……………………..	xvii
CASTAWAYS …………………………………………………..	1
HOLIDAY OUT …………………………………………………...	23
MEOWLESS …………………………………………………….	43
About the Translator ……………………………………………..	60
Critical Reaction to the Plays …………………………………….	61

ABOUT THE PLAYWRIGHT

Among the generation of Spanish playwrights collectively known as the "Marqués de Bradomín" group, Itziar Pascual stands out for her eclectic, postmodern theatre as well as her leadership among the young, female playwrights of Spain. Born of Basque origin in 1967, Pascual received her professional training in Madrid, where she currently lives and works. She holds dual degrees in Journalism (Universidad Complutense, 1990) and Performing Arts (Real Escuela Superior de Artes Dramáticas, 1996). Presently, she is a professor of literature and theatre at the RESAD. Pascual is one of the more prolific playwrights of her generation, having written more than twenty-five plays since the early 1990's. Most of her works have been published and/or staged in both Spain and abroad with much success. In the last few years, she has garnered some of the most prestigious national theatre awards, among them the Premio Marqués de Bradomín and the Premio María Teresa León.

Pascual's plays address a wide-range of topics that appeal to a broad audience. A recurring theme is that of memory, which is examined in *Memoria* (*Memory*, 1993), *El domador de sombras* (*The Shadow Tamer*, 1996), and *Pere Lachaise* (2003). The playwright also cleverly gives a revisionist twist to ancient myths, as demonstrated in *Las voces de Penélope* (*Penelope's Voices*, 1998), *Electra* (2001) and *Salomé* (2002). Furthermore, many of Pascual's works explore contemporary issues such as domestic violence (*Pared [Wall]*, 2004), exile *(Jaula [Cage]*, 2004) and war (*Palabras contra la guerra* [*Words Against War*], 2003).

Pascual's plays have an unconventional flair due to their highly fragmented nature and minimalist style. Poetic, and at times disturbing, her dialogues echo the vibrant language of today's generation. The strong influence of music adds to the lyrical character of her works.

In 2001, Itziar Pascual co-founded the Asociación de Mujeres en las Artes Escénicas de Madrid (AMAEM) *Marías Guerreras* (The Madrid Association of Women in the Dramatic Arts), a pioneering organization for women in all areas of Spanish theatre.

Susan Berardini

ITZIAR PASCUAL
Photo by Rafael Roa

Castaways, performed in Madrid in 2006. From left to right (standing): Anabel Ochoa, Nieves Mateo, Marta Navas. From left to right (kneeling): Angela Gómez, Cristina Regueira, and Isabel Ameyugo. Photo by Eduardo Sánchez de Rojas.

Castaways, performed in Madrid and directed by Victoria Paniagua, 2006. From left to right: Marta Navas, Anabel Ochoa, Isabel Ameyugo, Ángela Gómez, Nieves Mateo and Cristina Regueira. Photo by Eduardo Sánchez de Rojas.

Cast of *Castaways*. From top to bottom, left to right: Nieves Mateo, Isabel Ameyugo, Itziar Pascual (playwright), Victoria Paniagua (director), Cristina Izquierdo, Anabel Ochoa, Marta Navas, Lola Cantero and Ángela Gómez.
Photo by Eduardo Sánchez de Rojas.

Ángela Gómez and Anabel Ochoa in *Castaways*, Madrid, 2006. Directed by Victoria Paniagua. Photo by Eduardo Sánchez de Rojas.

Georgina Richardson as Soledad in Itziar Pascual's *Holiday Out*. American premiere, Cabaret Theatre, New Brunswick, NJ, April 2002. Dir. Michael Schlick. Photo: Phyllis Zatlin.

DIRECTOR'S NOTE

It was an honor to direct the United States debut of the Spanish playwright Itziar Pascual's *Holiday Out*, translated to English text by Phyllis Zatlin. The one-woman piece showcases Pascual's unique style of creating a complex character whose ideals are questioned in the face of personal turmoil. Discovering the intricacies of Pascual's character produces a challenge and a thrill for both the actor and the director by allowing the character development to take precedence over the staging or other technical aspects of the production.

Soledad, which means loneliness, is returning home from her one-week vacation by the sea, which was a misguided attempt to rediscover herself after the loss of her demanding mother. She arrives home, unrested, only to find that the airline has lost her suitcase. As she waits for the arrival of her dear belongings, she converses with herself, the airline attendant, the security guard, and even her prodigal suitcase as if they were all part of her own fragmented psyche. She equates the loss of her luggage to the loss of her mother. Soledad eventually finds that the clarity she was searching for was not to be found on a sunny beach in Spain, but somewhere much closer to home.

Holiday Out translates seamlessly to an American audience due to the innate human struggle of the character in the face of a universal dilemma. In a question and answer session after the debut of the piece, I asked Itziar about the significance of the title, *Holiday Out*. She replied with a divulging grin that it was a satire on the famous American hotel chain. For me, the illusionary simplicity of this piece was summed up with that one simple response hidden behind that calculated smile.

Michael Schlick
Associate Producer, 2001-2002
Cabaret Theatre

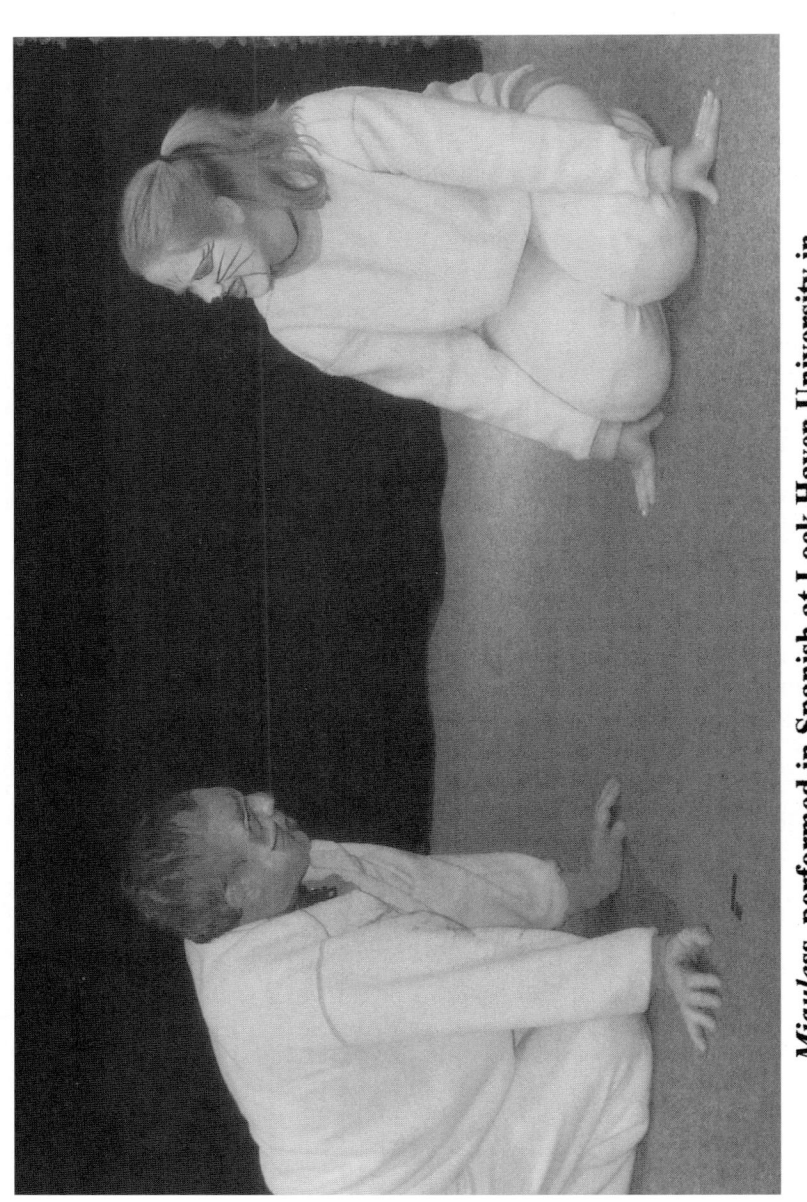

Miauless, performed in Spanish at Lock Haven University in 2004, directed by Peter Podol. Peter Podol and Andrea Wheeler. Photo by Enrique Herrera.

A NOTE ON THE PLAYS

Itziar Pascual is among the most important and active contemporary dramatists of Spain. Her rich and varied work illustrates her dedication to the craft of playwriting and to the promotion of theatre studies, feminism, and contemporary theatre production. Pascual's plays demonstrate a profound commitment to giving voice to the silenced, exploring experiences of solitude and misunderstanding, and examining the operations of power and privilege. The three plays in this volume are exemplary not only of the thematic intensity of her work, but also of her eloquent use of dramatic design as well as her ability to engage audiences. From her attention to theatrical rhythm to her innovative use of fragmentation, music, and space, Pascual successfully employs multiple elements of dramatic discourse, expertly maximizing the sensorial potential of theatre.

Holiday Out (Postcard from the Sea) is a monodrama for one female character, Soledad, who has returned from vacation to find that her luggage has been lost. From this familiar airport situation, Pascual has created an amusing yet thought-provoking monologue that artfully interweaves social commentaries on materialism, inequality, and gender roles. Soledad's observations are both lively and contemplative as various interlocutors are cleverly evoked through both her words and silences. Soledad's "interactions," reactions, and reflections lead the audience on a rollercoaster ride of human emotions. From her frustration at having to justify the fact that she is a single, unmarried woman traveling alone, to her philosophical questioning regarding personal identity and the monotony of daily routine, Soledad's monologue is genuinely humorous and charming.

By far the most serious and poignant of the three works, *Castaways* explores the theme of political exile. Each scene presents the interaction between a different pair of women, identified only as "A" and "B", who are often contrasted by age or social class. The ten sequences portray the somber consequences of war, violence, and exile: familial disagreement and separation, politically motivated aggression and betrayal, the search for safe haven, and the struggles of living as social and cultural outcasts. *Castaways* is emblematic of Pascual's commitment to giving voice to the historically silenced. While the characters are often at odds with one another or unable to communicate, the last scene, appropriately titled "Memory," concludes the play with a hopeful ending. While Pascual dedicates the play to the forgotten, exiled women of the twentieth century, her use of the generic "A" and "B" instead of character names evokes unequivocal solidarity with people facing similar adversity today.

The final dramatic piece in the collection, *Meowless*, is a light-hearted, open-ended play that explores the basic human (and animal) need for understanding, respect, and independence. *Meowless* presents the relationship between a teenage girl and Meowless, the cat. The protagonists' interaction is complemented by two other characters, one human, Veterinarian, and the other feline, Kitty. Ironically, even though the Girl feels that her off-stage parents do not grant her enough autonomy; she fails to recognize Meowless' similar need for independence. After a brief stay at the Girl's home, Meowless chooses to renounce his life of leisure and comfort in order to return to his vagabond life as a stray cat. The young Veterinarian consoles the Girl, helping her to comprehend that Meowless' needs and desires are similar to her own. Certain to make audiences laugh, *Meowless* is a wry comedy that invites the spectator to reassess not only the growing pains of adolescence, but also the fluid dynamic of human/animal relationships.

Holiday Out, Castaways, and *Meowless* exemplify the rich, innovative nature of Itziar Pascual's theatre. Phyllis Zatlin has artfully translated Pascual's complex and talented dramaturgy with expert insights to cultural details and linguistic nuances, highlighting the playwright's graceful style and evocative language—at times colloquial and direct, and at others highly poetic. Entertaining, engaging and provocative, these plays explore universal themes that will certainly appeal to a wide audience.

Jennifer A. Zachman
Saint Mary's College

CAUTION: Professionals and amateurs are hereby warned that *Gone Astray: Castaways, Holiday Out* and *Meowless*, being fully protected under the Copyright Laws of the United States of America, the British Empire, including the Dominion of Canada, and all other countries covered by the Pan-American Copyright Convention and the Universal Copyright Conventions, and of all countries with which the United States has reciprocal copyright relations, are subject to royalty. All rights, including professional, amateur, motion picture, recitation, public reading, radio and television broadcasting, and the rights of translation into foreign languages, are strictly reserved. Particular emphasis is laid on the question of readings, permission for which must be secured in writing. No part of this publication may be reproduced, stored in a retrieval system, or transmitted, in any form or by any means, without the prior permission in writing of ESTRENO Plays.

Inquiries regarding permissions should be addressed to the author through :

D. Alfredo Carrión Saiz
Director de Artes Escénicas y Musicales
Sociedad General de Autores y Editores
Fernando VI, 4
28004 Madrid, SPAIN
Phone: 011-34-91-349-96-86   Fax: 011-34-91-349-97-12
E-mail: acarrion@sgae.es

or through the translator:

Phyllis Zatlin
E-mail: pzatlin@hotmail.com
Phone: 1-732-238-5729 or 1-920-823-2013

Varadas (*Castaways*) was first staged in Madrid in 2006 under the direction of Victoria Paniagua.

Holliday Aut (*Holiday Out*) premiered in Madrid in 1996 at the Muestra Internacional de Teatro Alternativo, directed by Adolfo Simón. It received its American premiere in April 2002 with performances at Rutgers University in New Brunswick, NJ, produced and directed by Michael Schlick.

Miauless (*Meowless*) was first presented in 1997 in Madrid as a staged reading at the Real Escuela Superior de Arte Dramático, directed by Natalia Menéndez, as part of the cycle "Detrás de las sombras." It premiered in the United States at Lock Haven University in 2004, directed by Peter Podol.

Itziar Pascual's

CASTAWAYS

(*Varadas*)

Translated from the Spanish

by

Phyllis Zatlin

From sea to sea, the war between them,
far deeper than the sea.

Antonio Machado

For all those women in the twentieth century who sailed on the ships of the forgotten. And, in particular, to my mother and grandmother.

Itziar Pascual

1. EXCHANGES

An inhospitable, undefined space. Dark and cold. On stage, A and B. A is a young woman, dressed in dark clothing. B is a young woman, dressed completely in black. It is raining.

A: Is anyone there? Who is it? (*Silence.*) Is that you?

B: What do you want?

A: Oh! Are you... the Hyena?

B: Who sent you?

A: I'm here for my mistress.

B: And what does your mistress want?

A: To leave the country. A safe conduct. And a guide to the border.

B (*With a loud laugh*): And what does she have to offer?

A: She's offering money.

B: Who wants devalued currency?

A: She's offering a lot of money.

B (*Aggressively*): I'm not going to say it again.

A: She has bank stock.

B: I'm in a hurry. Doesn't your mistress have anything of value?

A: She has jewelry.

B: What kind?

A: Strands of pearls, necklaces of coral, amber, amethyst, jade, agate, set in silver–

B: Don't insult me. (*Crosses to exit.*)

A: Rubies, sapphires, emeralds and diamonds, set in platinum and white gold.

B: That's better. (*She stops walking.*) Anything more?

A: More?

B: Paintings? Silverware? Ivory and ebony carvings? What about tea sets made in Czechoslovakia? And Persian rugs? Velvet curtains? Chinese ceramics? Swiss fountain pens? Or fancy jewelry boxes? And watches?

A: There's nothing left.

B: I don't believe you.

A: I'm not going to say it again. (*Pause.*) It's a good deal.

B (*Laughing nervously*): No. It's not enough.

A: What do you want, Hyena?

B: Everything.

A: That's all that's left. She's had to sell it secretly, bit by bit.

B: She still has the house.

A: It's mortgaged. Two mortgages.

B: There's still the return.

A: What do you mean?

B: If she returns, she'll work for me. She'll be my servant. In exchange, I'll open the border for her.

A: Work for you? For the Hyena? Are you crazy? That's the world upside down!

B (*Sharply*): You said it. We're the ones on top now. The ones who open doors. The ones who save people from a certain death. A life is worth nothing. But saving one costs a lot. Send that message to your mistress. With my kindest regards. (*Exits.*)

A: Don't expect her to accept a deal like that.

BLACKOUT

2. PASSPORT

A comfortable dining room. Table, chairs, a painting or two, a wilted bouquet of flowers, an embroidery frame. On the floor there are two sturdy suitcases, fully packed. It is late afternoon. On stage, A and B. A is a middle-aged woman with a strong build and dark complexion. B is a fragile-looking middle-aged woman with thin legs, pale skin and light-colored eyes.

A: Will it take much longer?

B: No. (*Pause.*) By now should be...

A: Ah.

B: I've been taking pictures. You'll see. Of the back closet. Of the rocking chair. I took lots of the chest of drawers. Poor drawers, so empty. Well... I couldn't buy–

A: What time is it?

B: Oh... I didn't have time. I should have remembered. The clothes will be ruined. They'll rot away. First there will be tiny little holes. Then bigger and bigger ones. I don't like the smell in the drawers, on the hangers, but there's no other way. They mask it with lavender, but that does no good. It smells just as bad. Reminds me of the end of summer.

A: Are you sure? Should have been here...

B: You never know. You have to plan ahead. They're there, into your things, into your life, prowling around, in the back of the closet, in the heart of... And one day they gobble it all up. How do they do that? I mean... Do they swallow, or chew, or eat? Do they gulp it down in one bite, without savoring the taste? Or are they like cows, chewing their cud? On the other hand, in wood they leave labyrinths, corridors, immense, interconnecting tunnels—

A: What's this? Look. Here, here. Don't you see it? Run, get me a rag. It's... Run. I can't get it off. It's dripping.

B: I didn't tell you. A vase broke.. Before, in such a hurry... It's the water from...

A: It's dripping from one or the other. Look, it's coming from there. You must not have shut it properly. That's it. (*Silence.*) What vase?

B (*Compulsively, in a rush*): Forget it, what's done is done, what does it matter, it's all the same, just think, I didn't get a picture of it, I forgot the vase...

A: You know what your problem is? You spent your whole life collecting things. Collecting, yes, collecting. Putting aside, saving, filling space and even the air with so much... "I couldn't just leave it there," you said. Every day, something more. Cramming the rooms with meaningless, useless, worthless stuff. And my few little things, they disappeared. The mystery of things that break by themselves. The case of the suicidal vase. But your things, not at all. They grew and grew overnight. "I couldn't just leave them there," you insisted. And now what? What are you going to do?

(*Silence. B stands, looking down.*)

C (*Voice from offstage*): Your passport is being held until further notice. You cannot leave the country. Until further notice. Your sister can board if she wishes. Take it easy, ma'am. You are talking to the person in charge. You two decide. We're casting off in fifteen minutes. One suitcase per person. Yes, one. Alright. Have a good trip, ma'am. (*Silence.*) Did you know that your suitcase is dripping?

BLACKOUT

3. FAREWELL

A comfortable living room. Table, chairs, a small sideboard. A and B are on stage. A, a middle-aged woman, is wearing a purple skirt and a short, loosely woven knit housecoat. B, also middle-aged, wears a knit sweater and skirt set of moss green and low-heeled black shoes.

A: So everything is decided. Everything. I've checked out the pantry, the cupboard, the little attic over the kitchen, the built-in closets in the front hall. Even the storeroom. Just think, I even had time to go into the storeroom. Everything's in order. I've counted everything. I wore myself out, and that's the truth. We lack for nothing. In the pantry we have olive oil and sunflower seed oil; lentils, chickpeas in glass jars and in bags, and a couple bags of kidney beans, just in case, although I know you don't much like kidney beans; and rice, rice until you're sick of it. But a rice dish always comes in handy. There are cans of peas, corn—who would have thought that people would start eating what used to be just for pigs—and those special red peppers, two boxes of them. You won't believe it, but there's even a can of asparagus that we didn't use at Christmas. You remember that fancy white asparagus? Well, we still have a can of it. Wait, I've forgotten something. What was it? Oh, yes, flour. How long have we had it? Well, what doesn't kill you makes you fat. It's in the pantry. Then—

B: The last boat leaves tonight. Then they stop running. This is the last one. (*Pause.*)

A: So? What are you saying? What are you telling me?

B: Just what I said. Afterwards there will be no escape. We won't be able to leave.

A: And who wants to leave? Haven't you been listening? Sometimes you say things that... Oh, well. Let me continue. In the cupboard, the one we keep locked, you can see that somebody has been rummaging around, maybe the maid, who knows, I imagine it was the maid because, who else could it be? You have to keep an eye out.

B: I've bought two tickets. There weren't many left, I couldn't bargain for them. But I have two.

A: Have you lost your mind? What on earth made you go to the port? You could have been mugged. You hear me? And what do we want two tickets for, for what? You'll have to return them. Send the maid to turn them in, don't take the risk yourself. Don't even think of it.

B: We have to go. Here we're alone, defenseless against what might happen.

A: Here we're safe. At home, in my home. You want me to leave everything, just like that? Here I put in years of effort, of work, of sacrifice. Payment by payment, month by month. And you want me to run away? If we go, who will protect the house? We have locks, dead bolts, we can close the windows, it's a thick door, we can shut outselves in here, but if we go away... Who will protect it from thieves, from strangers, from...? They'll strip it bare!

B: Even if we stayed, we could not protect it. We have to go.

A: They'll get in over my dead body.

B: That they will. (*Pause.*) I didn't mean... I'm sorry. No one can guarantee safety here any more.

A (*Nervously*): You're telling me... you're telling me that...?

B: I'm telling you that's I'm going. And I want you to come with me. (*Pause.*)

A: Think about it. You would never have had this. A home like this, with balconies, sunlit. Now it's coercion. My home or you. What a coincidence, two tickets left, to go away, the two of us, who knows where, who knows with whom, nowhere, to die of hunger at the border, to die of shame when some dirty man searches us, to die of sorrow when we see how our world is vanishing, but we do have the tickets. So everything is decided. Right?

(*B does not answer.*)

BLACKOUT

4. BETRAYALS

An apartment, in disorder. Books on the floor, a man's clothing strewn about. On stage, A and B. A is a young woman, a student. She wears blue jeans and a long knit sweater of bright colors; her hair is in a braid. B is an elderly woman. She wears a black jacket and several strands of pearls; her hair is pulled back in a bun. B is looking through papers and documents; she scans them, puts them in piles, then tears them into little pieces.

A: You should go. If you stay, they will have no regard for your age or your family's reputation. Please go.

B: I warned him. I don't keep quiet, and certainly not in this kind of situation. He was almost finished with his degree, just a few more courses. Than he could teach at the university. A secure, respected job. Later he'd have time to write, but no—

A: They have dragnets, checkpoints, army patrols; they're arresting people. Just forget this and get out of here.

B: Those union people duped him. They invited him to secret meetings, they got him to write for them. Why didn't I realize it in time? Those people sucked his brain, took advantage of his good heart, they got him involved in their shady affairs, they filled him with rancor, with bitterness toward his family, his own kind!

A: I'll take care of everything. You have to trust me. I'm on your side, believe me. They'll find you here, they're looking for him; maybe he's managed to escape.

B: He stopped coming home to eat, his visits were further and further apart, he was avoiding us. He said that he was busy, classes, exams. Excuses. And when he did come, he was distracted; his mind was somewhere else, far away. I understood that the problem was politics, blasted politics. Instead of studying, call for a strike. (*Holding a piece of paper in her hand, she tears it to bits.*) What have they done for him? How have they helped him? What was in it for him?

A: What did you expect? That he'd sit on his hands? That he'd draw the curtain so he wouldn't see the arrests? That he'd say nothing? That he'd read the newspapers that cover up the truth? Or worse, that he'd become a cynic? Did you expect him to say, "If they arrest them, there must be a reason" and just sit there stirring his coffee? That he'd accept silence and coercion?

B: He should never have left Berenice. I told him,. but he didn't listen. Berenice was a cultured, sensible girl, with her feet on the ground. A delightful young woman, from a good family, an important, influential family. She would not have consented, she wouldn't have tolerated this nonsense, this disorder, this horrible chaos. How can he live in this chaos?

A: It's the country, that's what's in chaos. But if you mean the apartment, I find it changed. For the better. Now it has life, it exists, it's real.

B: He has to go back to Berenice, that would be best. Her family could get him out of the country. They have connections, lots of them. Their word means something. After all, it's just a misunderstanding, a youthful error, the awkwardness of a good boy, my boy. (*She looks under the clothes, in the corners, on the floor, throughout the apartment.*)

A: I like it better this way, spontaneous, alive. The old order was deceitful: a farce.

B: That trouble-maker is to blame for everything. That slut, that viper, that what's her name? (*Tearing up a pamphlet.*) That dreadful woman. She's the one who duped him. She took him away from Berenice, she introduced him to those clandestine groups. That...

A: Diana's like that. Too selfish, too much the center of attention. She never learned to keep quiet. They say she's been arrested. She'll betray him for sure. They will come here. Let's go!

B (*Looking in a pocket for a pack of matches. She takes a match and lights it*). How much did they give you to turn him in?

BLACKOUT

5. QUESTIONS

Early morning. Hallway of a middle-class home. A and B. A is a middle-aged woman; B is a teenager. A insists on bundling B up. B tries to rebel against the various layers that A is hurriedly putting on her.

A: Don't say a word. It's cold, very very cold.

B: Where are we going?

A: I'll explain later. Button up.

B: I don't like this sweater. It's scratchy. And it's worse when it's cold.

A: Don't argue with me. Where are your boots?

B: Boots? But, Mom, it's still night out. I'm sleepy.

A: Find your boots. And keep your voice down!

B: I'm not talking.

A: Shh. (*Lowering her voice.*) Come on! Get your things!

B: My things? Which ones? All my things?

A: Never mind. I'll do it. And your boots?

B: I've got 'em. What am I taking? I don't know—

A: And your scarf?

B: Have you seen my gloves? I can't find them.

A: Your heavy coat, not that one.

B: But I like this one better and the other one is still too big for me.

A (*Nervously*): Can't you hurry up?

B: I'm coming, I'm coming. But where are we going?

A (*Looking around, frantically*): Put on your boots! And don't make noise.

B: Will we be gone long? Wednesday I'm meeting Alina to study.

A (*Filling her pockets with some of her belongings*): Are you ready yet?

B: I won't miss many classes, will I?

A: Button up your coat and put on your hat.

B: Are we going to Grandma's? It's Grandma, isn't it. Is she sick? She got sick and you don't want to tell me? Why don't you want to tell me? Is she dead? What's happened to her? I'm not a child, you know.

A (*Grabbing B by the lapels of her coat*): Listen to me! We have to go, that's all. Stay with me, understand? Stay right with me no matter what. You may have to run. If they ask you questions, you know nothing. You know nothing about anything. We're going to Grandma's. Period. (*Silence.*)

B (*Repeating*): We're going to Grandma's. Period.

A: Period. And you know nothing.

B: Nothing.

A: Don't make any noise on the stairs.

B: I'll call the elevator.

A: No! They'd hear it throughout the building. (*She finishes buttoning up her coat and, for a moment, looks around the hallway of her home.*)

B: We're not going to Grandma's, are we?

A: No.

(*Exit A and B.*)

BLACKOUT

6. SENSITIVITY

Bare space. Wide, empty, perhaps with a wooden floor. Upstage, very softly, the sound of the sea and a light breeze. A and B. A is an elderly woman. A light scarf protects her hair from the wind. She wears sunglasses. There is a plaid woolen blanket over her knees. Seated on a comfortable lounge chair, she is reading a book. Next to her, an empty lounge. B is a young woman. Her hair is a bit disheveled. She walks around aimlessly. She is wearing several layers of clothes.

B: Have you seen where the...? I don't feel very... (*B seems to be nauseous. A keeps reading. Pause. B tries to look out over the horizon; she wipes her face with her hand. She takes deep breaths.*) I'm not used to it. Below it's worse. How much farther? Do you know? (*B is shivering. She tries to cover herself better, but her clothes don't help. She hunches over, crossing her arms. Pause.*) I can't stay. The air's too chilly. I think I have a fever. It's the nightmares... I can't sleep.

A (*Without looking at B, she reads*): "Her pallid face was flooded by the slow languor of her weeping. Her eyes, as intensely azure as the sea, let fall, one by one, the tears that he carefully wiped away, holding them in his hands. Nothing and no one can separate us, he said again, quieting her tiny sobs. I shall confront our family's lies, the pettiness of their selfish interests, the impotence of this miserable world that wants to keep us apart. And at dawn, I shall triumph." (*B starts to exit.*) Sublime. Magnificent.

B: Did you say something to me?

A: What sensitivity. What delicacy. What... Poetry. Sheer poetry.

B: I don't understand.

A: You don't have to understand. Just feel. Feel completely, let yourself go. Give in to sentiment, a boundless surrender. Boundless. Now do you comprehend?

(*B fights back another wave of nausea. Pause. B looks for a handkerchief in her pockets but does not find one.*)

B: Do you have a hankerchief? (*She sits down in the vacant lounge chair.*)

A: It's not a matter of culture or knowledge. It's a sensitive perception of the world, an infinite sensitivity... No, it doesn't depend on culture, it's something else. Now you understand. Did you notice? That way of describing: "as intensely azure as the sea." Poetry is like that. (*Not finding a handkerchief,* B *wipes her mouth on her sleeve.*) Great poetry, of course. Some people call shouting at a demonstration poetry. What can poetry have to do with machine guns?

B: Could you call a doctor?

A: There are always upstarts, mediocre people. Now more than ever. What relationship can propaganda have with poetry? Think about it: "as intensely azure as the sea." Do you understand?

B: A doctor, please.

A: Excuse me?

B (*In a murmur*): Please.

A: You know that you can't stay here. Rules are rules. It's nothing personal. I'm sorry. (*Pause.*) Go back to the hold. You'll be warm there.

B: Yes, ma'am.

(*B gets up, very slowly. A continues her reading. B has another wave of nausea. loses control and vomits. B spatters A's book. A, annoyed, gets up from the lounge chair.*)

B: I'm sorry. I've stained your poetry.

BLACKOUT

7. CROSSING

Darkness. Intermittent moaning. An atmosphere of cramped spaces, humidity, heat, human contact. Someone, at a distance, softly sings a lullaby. A and B are on stage. A, a middle-aged woman, wears a dark-colored shawl. B is a teenager. Her face is marked by sweat and fatigue.

B: Mom, how much longer?

A: Try to sleep.

B: My arms are itchy and I'm hungry.

A: You can have my shawl. Are you cold?

B: I feel sticky all over, Mama. Will it be much longer?

A: We must be about there.

B: That's what you said a long time ago.

A: Go to sleep. That's the best way.

B: That kid over there keeps crying. Nobody can sleep.

A: Try anyway. I'll make a spot for you, here.

B: When I lie down, I get seasick. Don't bother. How far have we gone?

A: We're almost there. Really.

B: It feels like we're not moving. There's no engine noise.

A: That's your imagination.

B: I'm telling you that we're standing still. It only rocks from side to side. Don't you feel it?

A: Today's boats don't move around a lot. It's not like it used to be.

B: Can't you feel it? It's not moving, Mom. We're stopped.

A (*Silence*): Lower your voice. They can hear you.

B: What's happening? I tell you we're stopped.

A: Now you stop it. Just in case, lower your voice. You'll make people nervous. (*Pause.*)

B: Let me have some water. Even if it's warm, that's okay.

A: Your brother finished it, a while ago.

B: Screw my brother. He should think about others.

A: Don't talk like that. You know I don't like it. Besides, there was only a sip left. (*Pause.*)

B: If there were a storm, we'd be moving, we'd be moving a lot.

A: You don't know anything about storms.

B: Of course I do. I'm sick of seeing storms at home.

A: At home. Well, we're not home.

B: I know, Mama. I know. (*Pause.*) You think it's an engine breakdown?

A: You're stubborn as a mule. Why would it be a breakdown? Tell me that.

B: Because it's not normal. Why would a boat be like this, standing still, stopped in the middle of a crossing? Or have we landed? What if we've landed?

A: You're making me nervous. Can't you stop it?

B: What if we were already in port? They'd have to tell us, right? Why doesn't the crew make an announcement? It's a short passage. Why did it take so long? What if they've arrested us? What if they don't let us off? What if they take us back? Now we can't go home... What will they do to us? (*A slaps B. Silence. Long pause.*)

A: I told you not to talk so loud. I'll stay awake, keeping watch. You sleep.

B (*With her hand on her cheek, pained*): You're sick, Mama. You don't want to see. And that's worse than having no home.

BLACKOUT

8. CHECKPOINT

An indefinite, closed space. Shiny tiles, a waste basket upstage, some extinguished cigarettes, sounds of voices offstage. On stage, A and B. A is a young woman, dressed in a uniform. B, an elderly woman, has white hair and shining skin; she wears a black coat.

B: You're going to give me information and careful attention, aren't you, honey? Yes, I can see it in your eyes, my dear. You're a good person. A good person and a pretty girl. Tell me, sweetie, where's the exit? I'm all turned around. Is it over there? Is that the way out? Sugar, I've always gotten lost, even as a child. I'd stop to look up at the rooftops, the sky, the chimneys, the grilled iron balconies, the windows on the tall buildings. And I'd get lost. One day—

A: Open your suitcase.

B: Yes, love. Don't worry. We'll be done in a minute. After all, this old lady, this clumsy old lady that you see before your eyes, doesn't have much, and mind you, I never disliked clothes. Dark cloth coats were my weakness. A good coat for taking a stroll, for looking at the roofs, the lit windows, for wondering what kind of life people in such a pretty building must lead.

A: What do you have there?

B: It's... my coat. My black coat for taking strolls. You must be tired, darling, so many hours here, so many hours working, on your feet, taking care of all the people who are coming to your country, such a pretty, friendly country, this important country that welcomes us like brothers and sisters, yes, like real family, because the attitude of your country is so fraternal, so generous, that it will take generations to repay you, entire generations filled with gratitude to people like you, such a lovely, sweet young girl—

A: Your coat's very heavy.

B: Oh, my child, my pretty child, it's that... It's that... They don't make coats like this anymore. The fabrics were different, thicker, a good material is a good material, honey, and the stitching, the finishing touches, the linings, all of such fine quality, a real marvel the way they'd last a lifetime. And fortunate, too, because of the freezing weather we've had the past few winters, particularly last winter. They say it's a curse, this cold that has taken so many, so many of the weakest ones. Of course here, in your generous country, my dear, fortunately you don't have these terrible problems.

A (*Taking out scissors, she cuts the lining of the coat. She feels inside the lining and turns the garment upside down. Out fall rings, earrings, a necklace.*): What's this? (*B does not answer. A picks the jewelry up from the floor. She tries on one of the rings. No one is watching them. She smiles.*) I'm different. I like rings. Not coats, but rings. (*Pause.*)

B: They belonged to my family.

A: Are you sure? Can you prove it? Where'd you steal them, you old thief? You know we can't let you into the country with stolen objects. You'll have to go back. What a shame.

B (*Speaking softly and slowly*): I'm begging you.

A: It's your choice. (*Pause.*)

B: Yes... They look very nice... on you.

A: Close the suitcase. You can go. (*She discreetly drops the necklace and earrings into the suitcase.*) It's the first hallway on the left.

(*B picks up her things and slowly exits. A is immersed in admiring the rings.*)

B (*Softly, to herself*): The bitch.

BLACKOUT

9. FORGETTING

A park bench. On stage, A and B. Both are young women. A wears sports clothing: blue jeans and a beige jacket. B, who is dressed hippy style, wears a long skirt and a scarf; she is rolling a cigarette. Both carry folders with notes. Long pause.

A: I don't understand.

B: But it's easy.

A: What does the milkman have to do with it?

B: It's a metaphor, an image. Yes, it's an image.

A: It's nonsense. Where have you ever seen a milkman making home deliveries?

B: They did it before.

A: Before? Before when?

B: Before. During the dictatorship. It was another time.

A: You sound like my grandfather. What about supermarkets? And grocery shops? And (*pronouncing very slowly*) corner stores? That would be in towns. In cities there were grocery shops for buying milk. Besides, I've never seen a milkman.

B: Well they came. They came to the house. Very early. They brought milk and yoghurt.

A: And yoghurt. Come on! What are you saying?

B: I swear. Ask your grandfather.

A: My grandfather says they had absolutely nothing. How could there have been milkmen?

B: So you'll just have to take my word for it. There were milkmen.

A: Milkmen who went to houses at six in the morning?

B: No. What is it, you're putting me on?

A: Why would I be putting you on? It's that I don't understand you. Did they go or didn't they? At six in the morning?

B: Well... I guess...

A: You guess? What you mean is that you have no idea. Just like me.

B: What a pain you are with that phrase. Maybe they went later. How should I know?

A: You see? So it's not so easy, that (*pronouncing slowly*) metaphor, that image. And if they didn't get there at six in the morning, why does it say they did? And what do milkmen have to do with democracy? Come on! What's the point?

B: Holy shit, because if it's a democracy, and someone comes knocking, it's the milkman.

A: Why is it the milkman?

B: Oh shit, what's with you today? You're really annoying me with that little phrase.

A: Yeah, sure. I'm annoying you. But it was very easy and now you can't explain it either.

B: Look. It's the milkman because that means they aren't coming for you.

A: Coming for me, why? Why would they come for someone? At six in the morning? I don't understand.

B (*Lighting the cigarette, she takes a long puff*): Look, forget it.

A: You see? It's not so clear, not so obvious. Besides, you don't have to open the... You're home, right? If you haven't done anything, why would they come? Thieves? Is that it?

B: Not thieves. Or maybe them, too.

A: So which is it? Thieves or not thieves?

B (*Taking another puff*): Thieves, paramilitaries, soldiers, police, and—

A: Para what? Police? Who called the police?

B: Nobody! That's the point. Nobody called them. They just show up, barefaced. They take people away. They take them away and kill them. If we didn't have democracy, you'd understand.

A: Bah. Democracy is a fiction. Let's go. I'm freezing. (*A and B start to exit.*) You've taken a liking to the professor, but as for understanding...

BLACKOUT

10. MEMORY

A nineteenth-century style bay window: curtains, high ceiling, little flower pots. It is getting dark and cooling off. On stage, A and B. A, an elderly woman, is seated in a rocking chair. She stares at the horizon with tired eyes. B is a young woman. She is wearing blue jeans and a linen shirt. Perhaps she is trying to give up smoking without much success.

A: And for three days and three nights, darkness was our only companion.

B: It was the last boat. The last one. Hundreds of women, old people and children were packed like sardines in the belly of that merchant ship. The humidity, the foul smell of enclosure, the feeble moaning of hungry children.

A and B (*In unison*): I shall not forget the humid smell. We had no water, no food. We gasped for air. The captain... (*A stops.*) Was it the captain?

B: Ordered the ship to retrace the crossing made during the day. And thus it was for three days with their respective nights.

A: That's it. Three days and three nights. Without knowing what was happening. Nobody explained anything. No one knew. Why? Only hunger and cold. Some were sick, and very still. In the belly of that boat. (*Pause.*) Your mother cried; she was so little...

B: Cried? She howled, you mean.

A (*Silence. Thoughtfully*): Sometimes? Yes. Sometimes she cried. She cried. Little sobs. Poor baby. She was hungry.

B: But another boat boarded our merchant ship. They arrested the crew. They arrested the captain. They took the boat to a neutral country. There they welcomed the last refugees.

A: The last ones... (*Pause.*) What does the news say? The radio doesn't work right. I can't hear it.

B: Nana... (*She looks for a pack of cigarettes in her pants pocket.*)

A: He deserved it. They deserved it. The cold, the hunger, the little children moaning... Some of them died. You know? Your poor mother. She was shivering in my arms. That's justice. (*B lights a cigarette.*) Not vengeance. Not really. Your mother knows that. I did not raise her to bear malice. (*Pause.*) What does the radio say? And the newspapers? Have you bought the newspaper? (*B takes a puff on her cigarette.*) If your grandfather were alive. He stayed here. He stayed here to fight. To resist. And I was there, with your mother in my arms; she was so little.

B: Nana. It's not a lost cause. There must be a recourse.

A: Lost? Your grandfather stayed here fighting, in the mountains, with the bombing, houses burning, bridges destroyed. Did you say lost?

B: The story doesn't end there. We'll go on.

A (*Looking at B*): I shall not forget the humid smell. We had no water, no food. We gasped for air. We were the last ones. The last ones?

BLACKOUT

END OF PLAY

Itziar Pascual's

HOLIDAY OUT
(Postcard from the Sea)

(*Holliday Aut
Postal de mar*)

Translated from the Spanish

by

Phyllis Zatlin

SOLEDAD (*Offstage voice*):
Dear Sea:
I can feel your presence from my bed in this hotel room. I know you're there. Outside. If I make an effort, I can hear you over the noise of the cars. That's why I've come to say goodbye and to remember you. To look at you quietly from the shore. To tell you that I hope to return one day. That I already miss you.

There are only a few of us left on the beach. The loyal ones. It's as if you knew that you belong to the old folks. They'll be here soon. As soon as it gets colder.

Old people accept the mild chill of winter. They give themselves to the present. They fear that this might be the last time they can feast on you with their eyes. That's why they dance to silly songs and eat every bite of the daily special.

This is the first and last year that I'm going to make you a promise. A promise that's not locked up like a message in a bottle. I shall listen to you.

I shall seek you where you are not. Under the florescent lights of the office; in the darkness of a train car stained with insolence; in the walk home under street lights, in a cold supper. I am going to take some of your mischievous spirit and give it to the boredom of my afternoons. Maybe that way they will seem less meaningless.

I'm not bidding you farewell; I'm asking you to follow me.

* * *

SOLEDAD (*Emphatically*):
B as in Barcelona, R as in Rumania, A as in Austria, V as in Valencia, O as in Oslo. BRA-VO. María de la Soledad Bravo Guimaraes. Soledad as in solo. (*She repeats, pronouncing with exaggerated clarity*) Yes, GUI-MA-RA-ES. G as in Germany, U as in Utah, I as in Iceland, M, A, R, A, E, S. Daughter of Valeriana and Enrique. Nine Buenavista Street. Phone number 573-1919. (*Pause.*) There must be some mistake. Are you sure? Yes. It looks like all the baggage is out. Yes, everything. No, not everything. My suitcase isn't. Are there more suitcases coming? Have you checked?

(*Silence.*)

But why? That's what I want to know, why me. Why does this have to happen to me!

(*Silence.*)

Don't you think that's too easy an answer? Chance. Coincidence. Fate. Are there statistics on lost suitcases per number of airline passengers? Funny. And how many of the lost suitcases are recovered? The majority of them? (*Alarmed.*) And what happens to the minority? Compensation. Yeah.

(*Silence.*)

Of course.

(*Silence.*)

If those of us who lose our suitcases are a minority, and an even smaller minority those who don't recover their lost baggage, then why do you say that it happens to a lot of people? That's misleading. Maybe we don't know how to travel. We should avoid the fuss and go by bus?

No. Nothing valuable. Nothing valuable for you, that is. For me, yes. Everything in that suitcase is very important to me.

(*Silence.*)

Right. Sentimental value. Anything you can't pay with a check has "sentimental value." How trite that sounds. Funny, isn't it?

And the claims clerk? If the clerk's not here, how can you put in a claim? This is just a form with my name and address. I wouldn't call this a claim. Well?

(*Silence.*)

No. No, no. You're confused.

(*Silence.*)

Don't bother. I think I'll wait. In case it shows up soon. On the next flight. Or in case they need me for more information. Just in case, for a while. (*Pause.*) You know, I'm coming home from vacation. Yes. The rain here is an unpleasant surprise. And the cold. And thinking that tomorrow I have to go back to work. Yes, that's the worst of it.

(*Silence.*)

When they bring it, what if nobody's home? I live alone. There's no doorman in my building. Yes, but nobody opens the door. They're afraid.

(*Silence.*)

No, I don't have any neighbors I trust.

(*Silence.*)

Would you mind? Looking to see if it's there somewhere. Yeah. In the storage area. Good. That's where it is for sure. Good.

(*Long silence.*)

You mean here? Let's see...

(*An even longer silence.*)

I don't see it. I am looking, but I don't see it. Well, that's that. No, no. No. Thank you for trying.

It's... dark gray, big, weighs a ton. It had a luggage tag and a sticker from the hotel. Holiday. Holiday Hotel. It's one of those big hotels, with a kidney-shaped swimming pool and chaise lounges. With a young, blond kid to hand out towels. One of those hotels that once you go in, you don't go out because they have everything right there. Well, actually you go out so you can say you saw something besides the hotel. But not for yourself... Well, maybe to stop hearing the aerobics instructors saying "Thirty more times" and seeing the German women doing just that.

(*Silence.*)

I recommend it. Not losing your suitcase, of course. But the Holiday Hotel. What a drag. Well. Nothing to do but wait. Don't bother. Don't worry about me. Can they be much longer?

(*Silence*).

Oh. Forget it.

* * *

SOLEDAD

(*One shoe on and one shoe off; sitting on a luggage cart with her carry-on bag wide open. Visible in the bag is a squashed stack of cinnamon buns. She takes out a package of cigarettes and matches. She takes a long, pleasurable first puff.*)
The good thing about smoking is that you stop thinking. You enjoy looking at nothing. Nothing, in the language of non-smokers, is smoke.

If I didn't smoke, I wouldn't know about it. "So, you reek of tobacco." "So, you're going to sound like a truck driver." "So, lung cancer." "So, how dreadful." That's what I say, Mama. No, I'm taking down the garbage. Or it'll start to smell. What a relief when I slam the door. Running down the stairs and out to the solitude of the square. The cigarette clamoring to get into my mouth.

That's when you discover that night in the city belongs to fugitive smokers and dog owners.

When I smoke, I think of them. The little old ladies who go out alone at night to lose themselves. To lose their keys, their coin purses, their identity... card. "I've lost my identity, you know?" "Have you seen it?" "No, I don't think so," I say to one of them. And she pretends not to hear me. "What a pain not to be able to find it," she says.

(*Silence.*)

I don't think so. They like to get lost in order to glide through the streets. Children, dogs and old people, what they like best is the street. That's why everybody wants to lock them up. So they'll forget their dreams and be obedient.

(*Silence.*)

She'd be delighted to be here, now. She'd be here and I'd be there. But smoking.

(*Silence.*)

(*Looking at a cinnamon bun.*) It looks worse than the liver my mother fixes. I'm never looking at liver again, not even from a golden calf. "So, it has lots of proteins." There are a lot of good things one can eat for protein. And if I protested, then she fixed more of the same, only breaded.

(*Silence.*)

You must have a supper break. You don't look like someone who skips meals. It's good to have a steady job. With a regular meal schedule. (*Picking up a piece of cinnamon bun.*) Me, on the other hand... Don't you believe it. I nibble more than I eat. (*Picking up another piece.*) To kill hunger pangs. (*Licking her fingers.*) Just a snack. It's clean, isn't it? Anyway, what doesn't kill you, makes you fat. Well, not me; I don't get fat. (*Using a cinnamon bun to wipe up the extra icing from the cardboard container.*) If I cut out starch, fat, soft drinks, sausage, nuts, chocolate and bread, I would be marvelous. (*Looking in the bag for a tissue to wipe her hands.*) It's what my doctor says. "Sol, you have to... " But I say to myself, you're going to cut out everything you can buy and eat? Not me. In the winter, when I work hard, I lose it all. Look like Ally Mcbeal. Say, is there a coffee machine here? Of course. If you have a supper break, you'll want your coffee and a drink. You're not somebody to skip a drink. To perk you up. And better yet with a cigar and a deck of cards. A little card game is good for the digestion. (*Slightly irritated.*) I know, I know. And your wife's at home, preparing heart-friendly boiled fish. I don't want any, I'm dead tired, don't be so insistent. What's a couple more pounds for the heart valves and the bathroom scale. (*Irritated.*) It's what you call an understanding husband. And if your wife fusses about standing in line at the fish counter and then wasting an hour in the kitchen, you bang the table and go to bed. To snore up a storm.

(*Very irritated.*) Look, the best thing about traveling is getting to know people. And I know where you're coming from. All the men who fill out forms and lose them five minutes later are the same. All men are the same. (*Extremely irritated.*) You think I don't know? You, you men who turn down boiled fish because you've got a full belly are the ones who lose suitcases, forms, travelers... until you make the rest of us lose our patience. Our patience. Not you. You fill your stomach with patience converted into "I don't know and I don't care." And sometimes it weights you down so that all day you go around hitching your pants up. And between the third gin and a belch, you make a sarcastic comment about how bad the country is and how badly everybody else does things, and they can just kiss your... The very ones! Don't raise your voice to me! I asked you not to talk to me like that! DON'T SHOUT!

(*Silence.*)

I didn't shout at you.

(*Silence.*)

I wouldn't be here if they hadn't lost my suitcase.

(*Silence.*)

Of course. I should go home. Then it'll never show up. That's what you'd like.

(*Silence.*)

And besides, I just want you and this airline, that I'm never going to use again, to leave me in peace. Some service! Until my suitcase turns up, don't even look at me.

How insolent.

You know what I say? That I don't intend to leave here without a solution. I got on that plane with my suitcase and I am not going home alone, tired, without a suitcase or a solution. You don't go away on vacation to come back like this. You go to shout at life and at the universe that you've been happy; that you enjoyed a perfect paradise for one week, that'll be followed by lots of boring, detestable weeks. You understand? You think that I signed up for that horrible miniature golf just to run into you? You think that I sunbathed with such dedication so that tomorrow I can show up at the office pale and with circles under my eyes? (*Picking up her bag.*)
No, sir. I'm not going to make it easy for certain undesirable people. For those who think they're the descendants of the Cid because they earn more money than the rest of us. Those who spout off about their new house and garden, with all the details: vinyl clad windows, whirlpool baths... No, sir. (*She takes out a Walkman, untangling the headset from the cords.*) Don't talk to me until I have my suitcase.

(*The audience hears the same music as Soledad. SOLEDAD begins to relax. She crosses her legs, enjoying the music. The Walkman in spurts drops in volume, followed by pauses. Then it plays again for a few moments. Finally it lapses into silence. SOLEDAD checks the tape, the batteries, the button and the headset, all to no avail.*)

Hey. Hey! If this is the claim department, then at least I have the right to make a claim! What? It's supper time? Or coffee break/supper time? You'd better leave so I don't find out the reason why you're behind that counter. Maybe you're the nephew of the general manager? The biggest stockholder? The lover of the general manager's wife? (*Scornfully.*) No. I'm sure that's not it. Your wife has enough with the fish you don't eat. If I were she, I'd flavor it with arsenic. Anyway, it has its advantages with the kids. "He's resting, so we will, too." Because you have kids, of course. And the story goes on.

(*Silence.*)

Look, it doesn't matter to me. I mind my own business. I'm at peace. I have my job, my apartment, I don't depend on anybody and nobody depends on me. I just want you to return what is mine. My suitcase. You know, a few years back the women in my building started checking me out for wrinkles and asking, "Why don't you get married?" And I casually responded, "To have to put up with a gambler or a drunk?" Like their husbands. They went running up the stairs, cursing all the way.

Hey?

(*Silence.*)

Hey!

(*Silence.*)

On top of being useless, he's deaf. You mute all of a sudden, or what? He can't hear me! Sure. His way of wearing me out. Not contradicting me, but doing nothing to find the suitcase. The customer's only right when he's satisfied. If he complains, he's an idiot.

(*Silence. To herself.*) Where did that man go. He must be eating his third supper. And the rest of us, condemned to wait. Well, I'm not budging from here.

(*Lights fade to **blackout**.*)

* * *

SOLEDAD
(*She has put on her shoes and is trying to tidy up her appearance.*)
Look, officer... That gentleman, if you can call him that... No... No... It's not like that. You don't have it right. Not at all. I yelled at him? I called him fat? I said he got the job by pulling strings? Look, officer... Officer... Are you a security guard, or a policeman, or an investigator, or a special agent... ? Don't pay attention to him, because he's twisting things. That gentleman ought to put more of his ample humanity into helping... You see? He won't let me talk! Aha! No suitcase and no voice either.

What did I have in my suitcase? I've already told this gentleman. Objects of "sentimental value." Clothes, cosmetic bag, presents... Well, presents. The kind you buy on vacation: souvenirs, little typical things, silly stuff... That's all.

It's a large suitcase, with wheels, hardshell, dark gray. It has my luggage tag and a hotel sticker... Yes! That's it! Exactly! Soledad Bravo Guimaraes! That wasn't difficult, was it? Where did you find it? Where? Well then it's not mine. I should go with you where? To headwhat? No, no. That's all I need.

(*Silence.*)
I don't care if the scanning machine, the German shepherd and the baggage screener are never wrong. There's always a first time, and I'm their first mistake.

(*Silence.*)

Officer, you're insulting me. I would never carry something like that in my suitcase.

(*Silence.*)

That some people are willing to do it doesn't mean I'm one of them. There are some people who buy books for the color of the cover, too. (*Silence.*) And besides, I've always believed in cooperating with justice. But you're not on the side of justice. You're just a guard under contract to protect the airline's rights, not mine.

(*Silence.*)

No, no, and no... One finds herself alone, without her suitcase, without rights, and totally ignored by a gentleman with serious hearing problems... (*Bluntly.*) You be quiet! How can I help it if he's deaf! It's certainly not my fault!

(*Silence.*)

I what? Pardon me?

(*Long silence.*)

Look. Let's take this one step at a time. Either somebody has put "that" in my suitcase or there are two identical suitcases that happened to be on the same conveyor belt and the one that turned up isn't mine.

(*Short silence.*)

What was that? Mr. Security Guard, tell this gentleman to speak more clearly or to be quiet; there's no way to understand him. He's too angry.
I'm a liar? I'm a drug smuggler? (*She grabs her bag and begins to handle it as if it were a blunt instrument.*) Is that possible? (*Waving the bag threateningly.*) To say something like that you have to have proof. Does he have proof? If this is a routine check, they can check me here, I've had enough with the lost baggage. Nobody's going to insult me routinely.
Be quiet, please! This mess is giving me a headache.

(*Silence.*)

You wouldn't have a Tylenol, would you? And why wouldn't you, when the job you're doing gives people a headache. And none of you even thinks about how our heads hurt. (*Pause.*) My mother used to get burning migraine headaches. She'd turn white from pain and cry because she felt helpless. She'd be so upset (*Looking in the bottom of her bag for a tablet but not finding one*) she'd go to her room and not come out. That went on all the years of her life. Every spring she'd go back to her family doctor. There'd be new capsules, modern tablets, the latest pills. All excellent. But they didn't do her any good. None. Then... "So, close the curtains!", "So, get me a glass of water!", "So, take this prescription to the drugstore!" Until one doctor, last spring, prescribed resignation. It was just a woman thing. My mother got angry. "For silicone and cellulite, there's something other than resignation, but for childbirth, or to keep us from tearing our stomachs and heads apart with pills, you just prescribe prayer. Who needs you when there are priests." I think the doctor didn't know what to say.

(*Silence.*)

I know that my mother doesn't matter to you, but it's relevant because my headache does have to do with you... With this horrible headache I can't be wandering around this airport. (*She continues looking in her bag.*) All I want is my suitcase, a Tylenol, a taxi ride home with a driver who stays out of bottlenecks, and a hot bubble bath. But first I have to have my suitcase. All I have to show for my week of vacation is the memory of a cinnamon bun that got squashed on the conveyor belt of this airport.

(*Silence.*)

Look, I'm trying to say this nicely, security guards are famous for getting nervous whenever somebody says no to them. However properly and politely. But I'm saying no. I'm not going anywhere with you until my suitcase shows up and both it and its owner are no longer under suspicion. You can call the police commissioner, or the supreme commander, or Saint Christopher, but I'm not going to budge. And that's that. Do what you please.

(*The lights gradually fade to blackout.*)

* * *

SOLEDAD
(*Standing, with a glass of water in her right hand. She takes a few sips. Then she tosses the plastic cup into a waste basket.*)
Thank you. I'm sure that will help relieve my headache. With these neon lights and those gentlemen—not that they don't have good intentions. But they're so crude. You, on the other hand, you're different. Such a nice haircut. (*Silence.*) Keeping your hair like that must cost a fortune. With that one wavy lock and the rest smoothed back. A cut that's neither long nor short. You go to the hair salon often?

(*Silence.*)

Ah. You want to talk about me. What does that have to do with my lost baggage?

(*Silence.*)

Maybe you don't know what to do with me or the situation? Don't be insulted, but your two colleagues didn't know either. To be truthful, to start talking about my life, just like that... It isn't necessary. If that's the reason, it isn't necessary. I've calmed down. I'm very calm. So calm that I've been here an hour and a half and my problem hasn't been solved. If I were nervous, I'd have started screaming a long time ago.

(*Silence.*)

That's what I get for coming back. I should have stayed at the Holiday, opening my door with a keycard and receiving messages on the television screen... Not that I got lots of calls, but I could hope.

(*Silence.*)

Look. Let's be frank, woman to woman. My head hurts, I'm tired, I can't go on arguing, and my cinnamon buns are gone. You understand? Good. Well, please, stop asking questions about my private life and my mother.

(*Silence.*)

(*With determination.*) I could spend the rest of my life talking about my mother. About her teased, purplish hair. I could tell you about her deep eyelids, cobalt blue first thing in the morning. I could tell you about her gruff voice, like a sergeant. And her flowered robe, going down the hall and making noises at night, headed to the bathroom. But will that help find my suitcase?

(*Silence.*)

I don't understand. I don't get the connection between my mother and my suitcase.

(*Silence.*)

I'm not talking to you right now, so let me finish what I'm saying.
You don't have any manners.

(*Silence.*)

Can't you stop interrupting? If he can't hear, how can he listen to anybody.

(*Silence.*)

I'm saying that you should stop butting in; I'm talking to this young lady and not with you. My mother loved grape. Grape jelly beans. She'd buy bags and bags of grape jelly beans and munch on them all afternoon while she was crocheting. Until her tongue turned the same color as the flowers in her robe. What? That'll help you find my suitcase?

(*Long silence.*)

Please. Put yourself in my place. In this horrible place. I'll explain it to you. First you get off a noisy plane, with people who won't let you into the aisle because they don't believe in taking turns, newspapers strewn on the floor, and some female voice saying "Goodbyeandhaveapleasantevening." Then you crowd onto a slow bus, where you become intimately acquainted with the other passengers, and they take you to a warehouse with bright neon lights that's been under renovation forever, with cigarette butts on the floor, carts that can't be unstuck, and conveyor belts. Any one of them might have your things. All of your things. On a screen they tell you which one.

Then, suddenly, a gate opens and they start to come out. Tote bags, suitcases, cardboard boxes, stacks of crushed cinnamon buns, a baby carriage, a bicycle, more cinnamon buns. But your suitcase isn't there. Your suitcase, your beautiful suitcase. It doesn't come out. You keep waiting while the people start to go away. The belt stops. Silence. You begin to assess the loss. "Good God, not my suitcase." And there appears a list of precious objects: the white linen shirt I just bought myself, the novel an old boyfriend gave me long ago, the brand new sensuous sangria lipstick... The special cleansing cream! Oh, no! Not my cream! Then, as I was cataloging it all, the gate opened again. Here it comes, for sure. It has to be in this second batch. A parade of objects. More stacks of cinnamon buns, a cardboard box. Oh, look! Finally! The stack on that flight that got squashed the most was mine. You can barely read your name that's covered with crumbs of angel food cake. Angel food. The angels must have the day off. At least mine does.

The gate just went down. We're alone. My cinnamon buns and I are alone. And now what? My things? My souvenirs? Where is the sand that stuck to my shoes? And the shells I bought on the boardwalk? And the postcards I wrote but didn't send because I could put them in any mailbox in my neighborhood? Where are my serenity and my peaceful days? Where?

(*Silence.*)

Look, young lady. During these happy vacation days I was alone, a solo act. I learned to savor my coffee and toast, solo; to smoke the first cigarette of the day, solo; to stretch out on the beach in the sun, solo; to put on my suntan lotion, solo; to read the newspaper, solo; to swim in the sea while keeping an eye on my belongings, solo; to eat something at an open-air snack bar that caters to foreign tourists, solo; to pick up my stuff and stretch out at the solarium by the hotel pool, solo; to look at my strap marks and the progress of my tan, solo; to get dressed for dinner, solo; to brush aside the greetings of the waiters, solo; to smoke another cigarette with my coffee, solo; to watch television and turn out the light on the nightstand, solo. Everything, solo, alone.

So I don't want to go home alone. I want to go with my suitcase; with my silly souvenirs and little treats. With those things that make life a bit more comfortable and a bit more my own. With that blouse that reminds me of a starlit night and my tranquil strolls, with the novel that made me feel so many new things, and with the cream that makes me more self-confident about going out into the street.

In my suitcase there are no valuable jewels, no checks, no works of art, no weapons, no documents that would jeopardize national security. The only thing in my suitcase is me. And I won't be myself until I find it. Now you know why I won't budge from this horrible room.

(*Silence.*)

Do you know that your hair reminds me of Tina Turner? I like her better that way. Don't you agree? I think it's attractive on her.

(*Silence.*)

It's that I don't trust you people! As soon as I go, you'll assess the value and that'll be it. So much money for so much weight. And I'll be more alone than ever, without my things, without my suitcase, without my souvenirs.

(*Silence.*)

Look, let's do something. I am sure that you're very good at encouraging people in case of air disasters, accidents, air traffic controllers' strikes, and things like that, but... Don't you think that my problem is petty and insignificant in comparison?

(*Silence.*)

Look, can we talk like friends? Good, thank you. Tell your bosses not to worry. I'm not violent or aggressive. It's just that I arrived with a suitcase and I don't want to leave without it. Okay?
(*Silence.*)

Come on! If they ask me, I'll tell them that we've been talking for hours, that you have made me feel much better, that you're terrific.

Think nothing of it. Happy to do it.

BLACKOUT

* * *

SOLEDAD
Good. It seems we can have a little peace. Let's see... (*Taking out a compact, she looks at her face in the mirror, touches up her make-up with a little sponge. Her motions get slower and slower.*) Horrible. (*She looks at herself again and holds the compact out in her right hand.*) You see, Soledad? It happens to you

every time. You expect other people to solve your problem and what they do is complicate it for you.

(*Silence.*)

What if the same thing has happened to it?

SOLEDAD'S COMPACT
Don't talk nonsense or they'll put you in a straight jacket.

SOLEDAD
Well why not? The suitcase has figured it out and said, "Go back? Why? So they'll put me up in the attic? Up there, alone, distraught, empty. Waiting for another trip. No. Better to get on a different conveyor belt."

SOLEDAD'S COMPACT
What do you know. Now suitcases decide their own fate.

SOLEDAD
It's better than being condemned to a year of waiting, longing for another week in a hotel where, between the clean clothes and the dirty laundry, you can be packed and unpacked.

SOLEDAD'S COMPACT
I don't know. I just don't know.

SOLEDAD
Don't you get it? The suitcase chose for itself. A nice, comfortable airport, surrounded by pretty flowers, with sunlight that merges with the sea instead of that neon that ruins your head.

(*Silence.*)

What? You have nothing to say?

SOLEDAD'S COMPACT
Well, maybe so.

SOLEDAD (*Snapping the compact shut*)
It went off by itself. That's all there is to it. But why didn't it say something to me? We could have escaped together!

(*Silence.*)

Like Thelma and Louise. And now where is it? Let's see what's on the list of arrivals. (*Staring at a fixed point.*) It must be nice, really nice. To stand in front of one of these boards with names of cities, times and gates. And decide. Pamplona, Rome, Alicante, Amsterdam. Just four, six, ten minutes difference. And if you miss a flight, you can always take a shuttle to Barcelona. One way, or round trip so you can come back and choose again.

(*Silence.*)

As I little girl, I liked to spin the globe quickly and stop it with my finger. That way I discovered exotic, surprising countries. I memorized the names of their capitals. And if my finger fell in the sea, I made it spin more quickly so it would fall on land.

(*Silence.*)

All my life traveling in my imagination and when I finally travel for real, my suitcase runs away.

(*With determination.*) I have to do something for it. Otherwise they'll pick it off of that nice, warm conveyor belt and bring it here. To the neon lights, the cab, the attic. If I allow that, it'll lock itself up in the closet and swallow the key. What can I do? (*She opens the compact.*)

SOLEDAD'S COMPACT
Don't ask me. I can barely get used to the idea that it took off by itself.

SOLEDAD (*Closing the compact*)
I have to play it cool. This doesn't happen to everyone. Or, if it does, they don't know it. Because if I tell them that it's not lost, that it decided to go away on its own, they'll send back the social worker. What are you going to do, Soledad? (*She opens the compact.*)

SOLEDAD'S COMPACT
Just think! You lose things you don't want to lose, but then there are other things that you can't get rid of no matter what.

SOLEDAD (*Closing the compact*)
Oh, leave me alone.

(*Silence.*)

It would be wonderful. An air line that checks in your insecurity. Well. They wouldn't take mine because it's over the weight limit. But to be free of part of it. Give a part of your fear to the world. Send your fear flying. (*To the compact.*) What'll we do? Don't say a word, gorgeous.

(*Silence.*)

What if I tell them that I found it? If I buy a suitcase just like it in the airport gift shop. I'll tell them that's that, not to worry, and my thanks for all their kind attention. I won't be going home alone. The social worker, the security guard and the claims clerk can relax: there's the vacation suitcase. Wonderful! (*To the compact*.) You see? The important thing is to make a decision. Otherwise you don't get anywhere. (*She takes the luggage cart and sets off with a determined step.*)

* * *

SOLEDAD
(*To her right, a dark gray suitcase. To her left, a dark gray suitcase, identical to the other one.*)
"What do we have here, what do we have here, what do we have here." Stop repeating that, please, you're getting me nervous from repeating it so much! Let's see. Let's see! I just want to know what my rights are. (*Opening her bag she takes out her ticket and boarding pass.*) Let's see... "The last call for boarding the flight is a minimum of... " No, that's not it. "Baggage allotment: first class, eighty-five pounds; business class, sixty-five pounds; economy class, forty-five pounds." Poor people have to pack carefully, right? Then... "Dangerous articles. For reasons of security, the following items are prohibited from check-in and carry-on baggage: explosives, ammunition, fireworks and flares." Sure you'd want them. "Poisonous, toxic and contagious substances." Ditto. "Radioactive materials." That's why the army has its own air force. "In accordance with Article 6, Number 6 (Regulations 192, adopted 4 March 1988), smoking is prohibited in aircraft in any area that is not expressly designated as a smoking zone." Well, that's true. Anything that is prohibited is defined clearly. But where are my rights? Passengers' rights, where are they? It's not fair. Totally unfair.

(*Silence.*)

Oh! And what do I know? Now there are two identical suitcases, both mine. Aren't you surprised that I went from having none to having two? And why do you think that I have an answer to that?

(*Silence.*)

Tell me why a suitcase and a stack of cinnamon buns, checked in at the same time by the same person at the same counter, get separated and the cinnamon buns arrive smashed and the suitcase disappears. Can you explain such a surprising phenomenon to me? Then why am I supposed to explain how a suitcase multiplies and becomes two. Mimetic reproduction? Osmosis? Virtual reality?

(*Silence.*)

I didn't do anything. I went to the lady's room to wash up a bit. Is there some international regulation against that?

(*Silence.*)

That's all. I came back, quite calmly, and found my suitcase here. By itself. I assumed that one of your company's employees had left it here.

(*Silence.*)

And now? Am I to blame for everything that happens in this airport? You're suggesting that I've gone crazy?

I'm not suggesting anything. I just want you to leave me alone. Let me go without bothering anyone. Is that okay with you? (*Pause.*) Well, it's obvious which is my suitcase, isn't it? (*Pause.*) And... And now you don't know. Then why did you ask me for so much information?

(*Silence.*)

You have it all written down, sir. Kindly look at your notes. Don't worry. I'll stay here. You decide.

(*Long silence. SOLEDAD whispers.*)

And you, where were you? You've had enough. Some homecoming. Now what? The social worker is all heated up. I think she should drink a quart of camomile tea and take a dozen tranquilizers. If you'd shown up earlier, you would have spared me the bit with your double. Maybe televangelists perform miracles, but suitcases don't multiply at an airport... The guard could find out what happened with that suitcase that looked so much like mine and that was accused of I don't know how many crimes... They're talking so loud you can hear them from here. I'll be! "It was a mistake." But before they proved that, I was presumed guilty. The guy from the baggage claims area, that lost and found department, has had his hands in his pockets the whole time. I think he must have been born with his hands in his pockets. He's going to hear from me. Let's see, what are we going to do?

(*Silence.*)

You know what I say? This makes no sense. You wanted to go away, I didn't want to be alone, and I'm alone, very much alone, you're here.

(*Silence.*)

We were both mistaken. I, wanting to cling to you, and you coming back. When we're alone, we cling to our silly objects. As a child, it's a rag doll that's nice to touch. Then we hide under our clothing: stretching the sweater that shields us from the cold. One day you discover that fear has stopped the hands on your watch. That sensation always arrives too late.

For me (*Gently caressing the suitcase.*), it came the day after. Your parents' death makes you vulnerable to time. It makes you realize that there will be an end for you, too, on one of the pages of the book you write from your birth.

Then you think that the best escape is racing forward. Placing your fingers on the globe and spinning it quickly. Until a word appears that sounds like a vacation. The view of a hotel where everything seems beautiful, impeccable, perfect. Like a smiling advertisement. But then it isn't true. You find out the last day, when you ask for the bill. You'd like to recreate the world of feigned happiness: the breakfast buffet, the little bottles of bath gel and shampoo, the magical order and cleanliness that comes after you've left the towels on the floor and the bed unmade.

After the false perfection there is a world filled with wrinkles. And as the mask falls, dear suitcase, we feel how small and useless we are.

I remember the Charlie Brown cartoons; the little boy with the blanket and his thumb in his mouth. His sad, frightened face next to the washing machine where his blanket is spinning.

(*Silence.*)

Look, suitcase. Maybe all of us try to find a way of breaking up that wait by the washing machine: a cigarette, a dog to take for a nighttime walk, an ID to lose, a Tylenol, a bag of grape jelly beans to eat slowly, a whirlpool bath in a comfortable house... Even if we don't know it, they keep us company.

Don't be afraid. The attic is waiting for you, and the office for me. The office, a house filled with dust, the dried out geraniums, the curtains that need to be tossed in the washer, the mailbox crammed with ads. And those three are debating, crying, doing nothing.
(*Silence.*)

Being frightens us if there is nothingness. As if solitude has to be cut into little pieces so we can cope. That's better than living life as a list of reproaches. If you come with me, you'll have to wait a year, locked up in a dark, small space. You have to learn to live with it, right?

(*Silence.*)

To live with my name.

BLACKOUT.

* * *

SOLEDAD
(*Traffic sounds. Cars, motorcycles, horns*).
Good evening. (*Lighting a cigarette.*) I want you to know two things. First, I'm going to smoke in spite of the sign with the crossed out cigarette. And second, I have the habit of writing down the car license and the taxi permit number. As a precaution. Well...

Yes, excuse me. We're going to 9 Buenavista Street. Do you have a light? Oh, well. Don't worry. I must have some hotel matches. The Holiday. A pretty hotel. I'm just back from vacation, you know. I was away. But I don't mind coming back. This is a nice place, too. Are you from here or from somewhere else? (*Pause.*) Don't answer if you don't want to.

(*Silence.*)

Maybe I'm distracting you in all this traffic. Turn down that one. Yes, the second on the left. No, it isn't one way. Well... Nothing's changed. Are you one of those cab drivers who are all for liberty but think liberal's a dirty word? Yeah, well just in case. My name is Soledad. Agh, what traffic! When the meter hits twenty-five, let me out. That's all the cash I have... Didn't I tell you I was on vacation? A week. Resting. The suitcase? What suitcase? I like to travel light. That way you have more freedom.

BLACKOUT

Itziar Pascual's

MEOWLESS

(*MIAULESS*)

Translated from the Spanish

by

Phyllis Zatlin

CHARACTERS

GIRL: A slender, pretty adolescent. She's at the age when ideas and affections become confused.

MEOWLESS: A curious, hungry and surly cat--until he stops being those things.

KITTY: A cat with soft fur and a fancy pedigree, but she has the heart of a mouser.

VETERINARIAN: A young man, dressed in a white coat. He has a great deal of patience, an attitude worthy of a Franciscan monk.

YOUNG WOMAN: Non-speaking role.

TIME

The period between a busy morning of shopping and a night of peace.

PLACE

An unidentified city where the sidewalks are filled with lonely people.

THE MEETING

At the doorway to a store; everything is red, white and gold. We hear the insistent tinkling of little bells, intermingled with children's voices. MEOWLESS is lying on a heap of orange peels, damp cardboard and old newspapers.

GIRL: Yes, Mama ... Yes. I've got the bag with the shrimp ... What do you mean there won't be enough? ... It's the same thing every year. *(Pause.)* Look, Mom, look. Do you see 'im?
MEOWLESS: Ummm! Doesn't that smell good!
GIRL: There, next to the garbage. Don't you see 'im?
MEOWLESS: You're carrying a lot of food. And your smell doesn't scare me.
GIRL: The cat!
MEOWLESS: Could you give me just a little?
GIRL *(Crossing to MEOWLESS)*: Hello... It's not doing anything. It's just a kitten.
MEOWLESS: What soft paws. *(Pause.)* And so big.
GIRL: Oh, he's so precious. *(Pause.)* Sure, he's a bit dirty but... Wouldn't it be wonderful if we could take him with us? *(Pause.)* Mama, please. Mama... Mama, let me talk, please... I don't interrupt you. If we leave him there, in this cold, maybe... *(Pause.)* Yeah. Lots of sheep for the manger scene, peace on earth and all that, but... *(Pause.)* Come on, let me do it. Just for today, Mama. Just for tonight. A little hot milk, a blanket. That's all he needs.
MEOWLESS: You're so warm. You can pick me up if you like. I won't scratch.
GIRL: But he won't be a bother! I'll take care of... *(Pause.)* It won't be any work for you. Just for tonight. Tomorrow he'll leave. *(Pause.)* I promise.
MEOWLESS: You're taking me with you?
GIRL: Let's go.

A BIT OF WARMTH

MEOWLESS has had his fur combed and parted to one side. He is sitting on a bright green and red plaid blanket. Next to him, a bowl of milk.

MEOWLESS: I need more eyes to see it all better. It's so pretty! And so big! And everything is warm and clean and smells good. But best of all, the very best of all, is this spot. (*He settles into an armchair.*) I hope it doesn't belong to anybody. It feels so good up against my belly. Much better than out in the street. Where it's so damp... Yeah, oh yeah. (*He adjusts himself more comfortably into the chair.*) Oh, that's good!
GIRL: Doesn't he look different? And he's so obedient. He didn't fuss at all when I gave him his bath.
MEOWLESS: And that... (*Looking over at his bowl.*) Not since my mommy went away have I had anything like that. It tasted so good.
GIRL: Mom, can I help? It's no trouble. What tablecloth should I use? (*Pause.*) Well, since we have a guest of honor... Do you want me to put the red candles in the center? Okay. Say, Mom... (*Silence.*) Do you think that he...? You know who... Could he stay? (*Pause.*) We're on vacation, Mama. Mama... Daddy, you say something, come on. Yeah, we'll see. We'll see. We'll see. Am I sick of that expression! I didn't say a thing, Daddy. (*Firmly.*) I didn't say a thing.
MEOWLESS: What's up?
GIRL: In this house, everybody has a right to an opinion except me. I just get to set the table. What? Shall I use the good silverware?
MEOWLESS: I don't like the sound of this. Are they talking about me?
GIRL: I am not being nasty! Just once I'd like somebody to think about me. (*Pause.*) I'm only asking to keep him for vacation. You're always saying I should have responsibilities. Well, I'll take care of him. (*Pause.*) Okay, cat. The two of us are on trial. (*Silence.*) Say, cat, do you have a name?
MEOWLESS: I look and look at them and I listen, but...
GIRL: If you're going to stay, even if it's just for a trial period, you have to have a name.
MEOWLESS: When she says yes, or no, I understand her. But...
GIRL: It ought to be a street name. Because you were a street cat.
MEOWLESS: Did you say street? Are we going out to the street?
GIRL: That's it! A street cat, a city cat without a home. Like the homeless. A homeless cat. Meowless!
MEOWLESS: Huh?

THE GAME

MEOWLESS is playing with a shiny, golden ball that he just knocked from the tree. The GIRL is sitting in the armchair, reading.

MEOWLESS: This is the life. Eat, sleep, play, lick yourself. It's not cold, it's not raining, the dogs don't chase you, and instead of taking food away from you, they give it to you. Every cat should be able to live like this. (*Pause.*) Would she like to play with me? I'll go see. (*MEOWLESS crosses to GIRL and begins to pat her with his paw.*) Hey? Hey? Look at me. Let's play.
GIRL: Come on, leave me alone. I'm studying.
MEOWLESS: What can be interesting about those papers. I don't get it.
GIRL: Sit still. Can't you see that I have to study? If I flunk the exam, you'll be back at the supermarket.
MEOWLESS (*Rubbing against her*): What if we went for a walk? We could take a stroll. Go out in the street. (*Pause.*) I already know this place. The long hall. The corners where there's always dirt. What if we went hunting? For little birds, maybe. Here there's nothing but a fly. And it's dazed and easy to catch.
GIRL: Don't bug me. If I don't catch up on chemistry, I won't pass. (*Pause.*) We'll play later, okay?
MEOWLESS: Did you see the pretty ball to play with?
GIRL: The tree! Don't even think about it! One more ball off the tree and we'll both be in the street. You give it to me right now and let me study. (*She takes the ball and puts it away.*)
MEOWLESS: All right. What a pain! I'm going to eat. It's the only thing I'm allowed to do in this house. (*Silence.*) Having food to eat is boring. This is no kind of life.

WHAT DELICIOUS FOOD

The GIRL and MEOWLESS are together in the room.

GIRL: You hungry, Meowless? You are? Let's see what we have to eat.

MEOWLESS (*Contentedly*): What are you going to give me?

GIRL: Da, da, da, dun! Deluxe chow! Catfood shaped like little cookies. Specially made for pretty cats.

MEOWLESS: Let's see. (*Sniffing it.*) This stuff smells the same as yesterday's. Why are so nervous? It's the same as always. (*Tastes the catfood.*) It's the same, horrible chow, like always. (*Pause*). Do you eat the same food everyday?

GIRL: Well, and I thought you were hungry. I'll just leave it there. I'm going to have supper. (*She prepares herself a sandwich.*)

MEOWLESS: Now that smells good! I get it. That's my real food. The stuff before was just a little game. Okay. Give it to me. Give it to me. Why aren't you giving it to me?

GIRL: Meowless, sit still. Your food's over there.

MEOWLESS: Let's play that I catch you and that you try to get away. Like cat and mouse. (*MEOWLESS jumps and knocks the sandwich to the floor.*) I won!

GIRL: Hey! What are you doing? Don't be silly.

MEOWLESS: Why play if you don't know how to lose? What are you doing with my food? (*Pause.*) I'd share my chow with you. But it's so disgusting, you wouldn't even try it. But you, on the other hand--

GIRL: Forget it, Meowless. Mama says that you have to learn that our food is ours and the chow is yours.

MEOWLESS: Yeah. The stuff that smells good for you and the stuff that smells disgusting for me. That's it, right?

GIRL (*In an authoritarian tone*): Now you know. That's your food. Take it or leave it.

MEOWLESS: Go on... Don't be like that... Just a little bit. (*MEOWLESS goes back over to the GIRL.*)

GIRL: I said no! Then you get sick and we have to give you medicine. What is it?

MEOWLESS: Sick, sick... I get sick when you say no. (*MEOWLESS moves away from her with dignity.*)

GIRL: Don't be angry, Meowless. Come on. It's good catfood!

MEOWLESS: I'm leaving. Let me alone. You eat it, all of it. I'm giving you my chow as a present. (*MEOWLESS leaves the room.*)

FULL MOON

MEOWLESS is alone. In the distance, sounds of happy voices, greetings and bells.

MEOWLESS: What a noisy night. They're all talking so loud, they clink their bowls before drinking, they hop about. They seem so happy. What's going on? And she... she smells so good! She even seems bigger than before. As if she'd grown suddenly. (*Pause.*) The more noise they make, the more I feel like sleeping. At least for a little while. (*MEOWLESS dozes off. When he wakes up, the noise has ceased and everyone is asleep.*) Is she asleep? (*Pause.*) She's not here! She's not home yet. Where can she be? Maybe something happened to her! She's been gone so long. (*Pause.*) Maybe she found another cat to play with, maybe she'll bring another cat here and throw me out, maybe she'll find one that's prettier and nicer and smarter and... Maybe she doesn't love me any more. They're like that. One day they do, and the next day they don't. When it gets cold, the streets are filled with abandoned... What was that? Someone's coming. If she's bringing a new cat, I'll scratch her. Because... because... just because. And I'll kill him. I have my pride. (*Silence.*) Of course she's never smelled of another cat. I've never noticed that. She always smells so good... (*Pause.*) Maybe she's doing it for me. So I'll have a friend to play with. So I'll have something to do when she isn't here. (*Silence.*) No. If she wants two cats it's because one isn't enough for her. I'm not cat enough for her. (*Pause.*) Here she comes! I'll pretend nothing's happened.

(*The GIRL enters on tiptoe.*)

GIRL: Hello, Meowless. What are you doing awake?
MEOWLESS (*Licking the GIRL's hands*): Where were you? Are you alone? (*Silence.*) Do you love me?
GIRL: Today's special. You can come up on the quilt. Go to sleep now.
MEOWLESS: Ooh. Tonight we're going to sleep together.

AT THE ANIMAL HOSPITAL

Neat, clean atmosphere. Light of bluish tones. Background music that supposedly is relaxing but that really makes everyone nervous.

GIRL: Relax. Calm down. Nobody's going to hurt you. The vet is very nice. It's for your own good.
MEOWLESS: I don't like this. We finally go out to take a walk... but not to hunt little birds. Shut inside. My stomach's churning.

(The GIRL glances at a magazine. A YOUNG WOMAN comes in quickly and sets KITTY down on the floor. The YOUNG WOMAN exits.)

KITTY: Oh, la, la. And who's this?
MEOWLESS: You smell good. Like my mommy.
KITTY: If I remind you of your mother, that's a bad sign. You all say the same thing. Don't you think that's a pretty old line?
MEOWLESS: Old? What do you mean?
KITTY: I see. You're a beginner, no experience. And a bit old-fashioned. You with her?
MEOWLESS (*Proudly*): Yes. She's wonderful. And you?
KITTY: Mine... She's always nervous. She's never home, and when she is, that's worse yet. Because she doesn't let me sleep. All night long she doesn't stop moving.
MEOWLESS: Have you tried staring at her? I think that calms them down.
KITTY (*Self-confidently*): I've tried everything with her. She's impossible.
MEOWLESS: And do you know... do you know why we're here?
KITTY (*Sarcastically*): It's your first time? You don't know about the veterinarian?
MEOWLESS: Vetewhat?
KITTY: Come on. You should work up some enthusiasm. Don't worry. It's no big deal. A couple of annoyances and then it's over. Not like the beauty parlor. There it's really nice and you come out so pretty. (*Looking at her nails.*) What beauty parlor do they take you to? I've never seen you at mine.
MEOWLESS: Me? They make me beautiful at home.
KITTY: Oh. (*Pause.*) Well. Today they didn't pay much attention to your appearance.
VETERINARIAN: Hello. Who's next?
GIRL: We are.
KITTY: Be brave.
MEOWLESS (*To himself*): Why is everyone telling me that?

COMMON FELINES

In the animal hospital. After the examination.

VETERINARIAN: Good! That's all. Now that wasn't bad, was it?
MEOWLESS: Big bully!
VETERINARIAN: Don't be so whiny. It wasn't that bad. (*Pause.*) This cat has real character. How long has he been living with you?
GIRL: About two weeks.
VETERINARIAN: And how's it going?
GIRL: At first, they didn't want him. Then I convinced them to let him stay for a while, on trial. Now I think they're pleased with him. He's easy to love.
VETERINARIAN: I mean him. How's he adapting?
GIRL: Well, I think. (*Pause.*) Sometimes he needs to unwind. He runs down the hall and jumps about. Then he relaxes and sits in the armchair. He falls asleep there watching the nightly news on Channel 2. (*Pause.*) He likes that a lot.
VETERINARIAN: You have to be patient with him, and respect him. Give him commands, explaining what's right and wrong. But, above all, never hit him.
GIRL: Why not?
VETERINARIAN: Meowless is a feline. A little, tame feline, but a feline nevertheless. If you attack him, he'll attack you. And with his temper–
MEOWLESS: Bring your hand a little closer, come on... I wanna taste those fingers.
VETERINARIAN: Pet him a lot. Physical contact is very important so he'll feel good and relax. Spoil him a bit. So that he'll... Ouch!
GIRL: Meowless! What are you doing!
MEOWLESS: He started it! He shouldn't have hurt me.
GIRL: That's bad! No!
MEOWLESS: And when he does it, it's okay?
VETERINARIAN: He's right. It's not pleasant to have someone handle you and measure you and then, to top it off, give you a shot. I'd bite too. (*Pause.*) Okay. We'll see you in three weeks, for the follow-up shots. Take care, champ!
MEOWLESS: Any chance you'll get hit by a truck?

THE DREAM FROM THE ORIENT

MEOWLESS is on the armchair. The GIRL enters, in a bad mood. Sound of a slamming door.

GIRL: Every year it's the same thing. Poor Grandpa, how he loved cabbage. And poor Grandma, may she rest in peace. How she used to cry on Christmas Eve... And if you protest, you're selfish and unfeeling, and you should get all sentimental because of the cider and the candied almonds. How lucky you are, Meowless, that you don't have to put up with it. (*Pause.*) Since you don't have a sad mother...

MEOWLESS: Mama? She picked me up by the neck and carried me places. Or she pushed me with her nose so I'd walk. (*Pause.*) Did you have trouble learning to walk? I always fell down.

GIRL: It's not as if we don't know who really brings the presents from the Wise Men. Even so. Put out feed for the camels, a sign with my name and the slippers on the living room sofa. (*Pause.*) They don't want to let me grow up. They don't want to get old.

MEOWLESS: I don't remember my father... hardly at all. He went away very soon. (*Pause.*) When I could stand up, all by myself, I went running to show him. But he wasn't there. (*Pause.*) He must have had other things to do.

GIRL: I want the Christmas season to be over. I want to see the end of these intimate festivities of happiness and peace, of frozen shrimp and easy tears... All those good wishes, coming from Pinocchio. (*Pause.*) The one who told the lies.

MEOWLESS: My sisters licked and licked themselves. All the time. Sometimes they laughed at me and didn't let me play with them. Because I was the only tomcat.

GIRL: Two years from now I'll be taking the college entrance exam. I'm not a little girl any more. But they don't want to realize that. (*Pause.*) Always with the same song and dance. "What time are you coming home?" "Your clothes look funny." "Who was that boy on the motorbike?" (*Pause.*) The first chance I get, I'm outta here.

MEOWLESS: Don't be angry. You have them. (*Pause.*) When they're not there, you'll miss them. (*Pause.*) I remember my mama and my sisters... I even remember my father. (*He begins to lick the GIRL very slowly.*)

GIRL (*Smiling*): When I was little, it was more fun. They took me to see the Three Wise Men ride into town, and throw treats to the children. Best of all was King Baltasar. He was my favorite, because he was the Black King. And they'd bring me a special ring-shaped coffee cake for Epiphany breakfast. We'd drink hot chocolate and eat the coffee ring.

MEOWLESS: I used to have special breakfasts too. Milk. When my sisters let me. Since they were bigger, they used to push me away.

MEOWLESS: You've already found him. (*Pause.*) Only to look for food? There'll be a full moon tonight. I can feel it coming. (*Pause.*) Can't you?
KITTY: Well... It's nice to find a friend from the old days. And so changed at that. You seem different.
MEOWLESS: It's the outdoor light. Shall we go?

(*MEOWLESS and KITTY exit together. **Blackout**.*)

GOODBYE CAN BE A HELLO

The GIRL is locked in her room. The VETERINARIAN knocks at the door.

VETERINARIAN: May I come in?
GIRL: No. You may not. There's a sign that says, "No human beings allowed." Can't you read?
VETERINARIAN: In that case, I'll leave. I don't want to bother you. (*He pretends to leave. Standing at the doorway, he counts to five on his fingers.*)
GIRL: Wait! Wait a minute!
VETERINARIAN (*Counting silently to three*): Were you calling me?
GIRL: Close the door on your way out. Please. (*Pause.*)
VETERINARIAN: Okay. I only stopped by to say—
GIRL: My parents sent you, right?
VETERINARIAN: No. (*Pause.*) Your cat sent me.
GIRL: You've seen him? Where is he? Do you have him?
VETERINARIAN: No. But locking yourself in your room and not eating is not going to make him come back.
GIRL: I'm not hungry. (*Pause.*) I don't want to see anybody. That's all. I want to be alone. They can just leave me in peace. Do you understand?
VETERINARIAN: I do. And your cat does. That's why he left. But you didn't seem to understand him.
GIRL: Why did he leave? My mother told me, "Don't get attached to him, street cats are all very strange. They don't know how to love." He had everything. And he went away.
VETERINARIAN: Maybe he, too, wanted to be left in peace. To be on his own for a bit. Like you.
GIRL: It's not the same thing!
VETERINARIAN: That's true. You gave him a bathtub, a bowl of cat chow, a plaid blanket, a colored ball, a couple of shots, and a box of kitty litter. And what did he give you? He left his world to live in yours. To live with your rules. And to love you. That's a lot.

GIRL: I loved him too! A lot. (*Pause.*) Do you think he'll come back?
VETERINARIAN: Very few do. Those that come back are battered, starved or sick. That's the law of the street.
GIRL: He had it so much better here than in the street. And he left. Such gratitude!
VETERINARIAN: You gave him whatever you could. But you can't change his instinct. You can't satisfy everything he wants.
GIRL: Like what?
VETERINARIAN: Like sexual desire. (*Pause.*) And freedom.
GIRL: If you think he's better off in the street, where he might get run over or eat rotten food, why are you are a veterinarian?
VETERINARIAN: He's not better off; but it's his space. Your house isn't the only possible home for Meowless. And your cat knows that. (*Pause.*) Think of it as having a friend stay with you. And then he left when your hospitality wasn't enough.
GIRL (*Pause*): Like E.T.
VETERINARIAN: Something like that. Only closer.
GIRL: But it's not true. I... I... (*Covering her face with her hands.*)
VETERINARIAN: Yes, I know. You hit him because he decided to mark his territory on your favorite shelf. (*Pointing at it.*) That one, right? (*The GIRL nods without showing her face.*) Well, that was not a good thing. I warned you.
GIRL (*Crying*): He was acting crazy... He started to snarl at me... He scratched my ankle... He'd never done that before.
VETERINARIAN: You'd have done the same thing. (*He crosses to the GIRL and strokes her hair.*) He doesn't do it to be nasty. He needs to let all other cats know that the space is his. Don't you have a sign on your door to keep the rest of us out?
GIRL (*Wiping the tears away*): Sure. But I let you come in.
VETERINARIAN: That's because I'm more animal than human. (*Pause.*) Well, now what? Meowless is where he wants to be. And with whom he wants to be. Okay?
GIRL: Okay. Thank you.
VETERINARIAN: No thank yous. I charge a fee, whether the animals have four feet or two. Aren't you going to invite me for coffee and cookies?
GIRL: And cookies? How about toast and strawberry jam? I'm hungry!

(*The GIRL and the VETERINARIAN exit the room.* **Blackout**.)

ALL'S WELL THAT ENDS WELL

MEOWLESS and KITTY are resting peacefully. It's that time of day when cats stretch themselves and people come back from shopping.

MEOWLESS: At first I thought it would be terrific. Eat, sleep, play. Then I understood. You don't choose your mother, or your sisters. You don't choose your territory. It's yours. And you belong to it. You mark it. And it marks you. (*Pause.*) Do you think she knows that?
KITTY: You think about her a lot, don't you?
MEOWLESS: Sometimes I dream that she stirs underneath the blanket and I'm looking at her. But when I wake up, she isn't there. (*Pause.*) And you? Do you...?
KITTY: Of course, dear. A lot. I miss those wonderful little cans of chicken, the soft sofa, the beautician's hands. Oh, so nice! (*Pause.*) But I fell in love with a cat who has no pedigree. (*Smiling.*) And I have no regrets.
MEOWLESS: Maybe one day we'll see her. Even if just from a distance. I think I'd know how to find her.

(The GIRL and the VETERINARIAN are out walking. The VETERINARIAN's face is buried in the many bags, of assorted colors and shapes, that he is carrying.)

GIRL: Look! Look! Meowless! Hey, Meowless!
VETERINARIAN: Where? Where?
KITTY: Your time has come. There she is.
MEOWLESS: She hasn't forgotten me. (*To KITTY.*) Run!
KITTY: Couldn't you ask her for a little can of...?
GIRL: Bye, bye. Friend.
VETERINARIAN (*Managing to free himself of the bags*): Was that him? (*The GIRL does not answer.*) Are you all right? (*The GIRL does not speak.*) Are you sure?
GIRL: Yes. Now I am.

BLACKOUT

ABOUT THE TRANSLATOR

Phyllis Zatlin is Professor of Spanish and coordinator of translator/interpreter training at Rutgers, The State University of New Jersey. A specialist in contemporary theatre, she has published numerous books, editions, and articles. She has been associate editor of the journal *Estreno*, contributing editor of *Western European Stages*, general editor of ESTRENO Plays, and member of the editorial boards of *Anales de la Literatura Española Contemporánea: Teatro*, *Art Teatral*, and *España Contemporánea*. She is an associate member of The Dramatists Guild. Among her published translations of plays from Spanish and French are José Luis Alonso de Santos's *Hostages in the Barrio* (ESTRENO Plays 12) and *Going Down to Marrakesh*, Jean-Paul Daumas's *The Elephant Graveyard*, Eduardo Manet's *Lady Strass*, Paloma Pedrero's *Parting Gestures with A Night in the Subway* (ESTRENO Plays 6), and Jaime Salom's *Bonfire at Dawn* (ESTRENO Plays 1) and *The Other William*. Stagings of her translations include *Lady Strass* (UBU Repertory Theater, New York City), Pedrero's *The Color of August*, (Pace University, New York City, and Loose Change Theatre Company, London, among others), *Going Down to Marrakesh* (Univ. of Missouri-Kansas City), and *Hostages in the Barrio* (Bridge Theater, Miami), and Itziar Pascual's *Holiday Out* (Rutgers and Ohio Wesleyan universities).

TRANSLATOR'S ACKNOWLEDGEMENTS

My sincere thanks to Iride Lamartina-Lens and Susan Berardini for their enthusiasm and invaluable help in making this play translation possible. My thanks as well to Michael Schlick and Georgina Richardson for bringing *Holiday Out* to life in 2002. And my deep gratitude to Itziar Pascual for writing these delightful plays and responding patiently to my questions in the process of translating them. I am grateful to the Office of the Provost at Pace University and to the Program for Cultural Cooperation with United States Universities for their support of this edition of ESTRENO Plays.

P. Z.

CRITICAL REACTION TO THE PLAYS

"The situation [of *Holiday Out*] is not only a humorous one, but also one that reveals a disquieting metaphor for the state of women…"

Eduardo Pérez-Rasilla
Reseña de literatura, arte y espectáculos, 1997

"*Varadas (Castaways)* is the story of so many women. Women who sailed toward oblivion. Toward exile. Toward emptiness. Women half-way between two continents, two shores, two lives… These women are in no man's land. Somewhere between ambiguity and loss."

Artes escénicas
Casa de América, Madrid, 2005

"Sole, the protagonist of *Holliday aut (Holiday Out)* by Itziar Pascual, returns home after her vacation traveling unusually light. Oh, so light! Her suitcase has disappeared, and she knows that after seven days in paradise, she has to face once again the everyday pressures, delays, habits, dissatisfactions with daily routine, and the burden of loneliness. Thus begins another voyage, a voyage to the depth of her heart.

Antonio J. Luna
ABC, 1997

"Airport waiting rooms have something in common with those of cold, impersonal hospitals; if the former lie between the heavens and Earth, a twilight zone, the latter is a delicate screen that can separate life from death; both places are on the edge, with their own rules and iconic codes, and are inhabited by two classes of people: those in a hurry and those who wait. In short, these places are a depot for the lonely."

Juan García Garzón
ABC, 1997

"Personally, this project has provided me with a two-fold pleasure: to continue betting on the Theatre of Madrid, and to work together with Itziar Pascual."

Adolfo Simón
Director, *Holiday Out*, Madrid, 1997

ESTRENO: CONTEMPORARY SPANISH PLAYS SERIES

No. 1   Jaime Salom: ***Bonfire at Dawn*** *(Una hoguera al amanecer)*
Translated by Phyllis Zatlin. Rev. ed. 2006.
ISBN: 1-888463-23-6 / 978-1-888463-23-1

No. 2   José López Rubio: ***In August We Play the Pyrenees*** *(Celos del aire)*
Translated by Marion Peter Holt. 1992.
ISBN: 0-9631212-1-9

No. 3   Ramón del Valle-Inclán: ***Savage Acts: Four Plays*** *(Ligazón, La rosa de papel, La cabeza del Bautista, Sacrilegio)*
Translated by Robert Lima. 1993.
ISBN: 0-9631212-2-7

No. 4   Antonio Gala: ***The Bells of Orleans*** *(Los buenos días perdidos)*
Translated by Edward Borsoi. 1993.
ISBN: 0-9631212-3-5

No. 5   Antonio Buero-Vallejo: ***The Music Window*** *(Música cercana)*
Translated by Marion Peter Holt. 1994.
ISBN: 0-9631212-4-3

No. 6   Paloma Pedrero: ***Parting Gestures*** with ***A Night in the Subway*** *(El color de agosto, La noche dividida, Resguardo personal, Solos esta noche)*
Translated by Phyllis Zatlin. Revised ed. 1999.
ISBN: 1-888463-06-6

No. 7   Ana Diosdado: ***Yours for the Asking*** *(Usted también podrá disfrutar de ella)*
Translated by Patricia W. O'Connor. 1995.
ISBN: 0-9631212-6-X

No. 8   Manuel Martínez Mediero: ***A Love Too Beautiful*** *(Juana del amor hermoso)*
Translated by Hazel Cazorla. 1995.
ISBN: 0-9631212-7-8

No. 9   Alfonso Vallejo: ***Train to Kiu*** *(El cero transparente)*
Translated by H. Rick Hite. 1996.
ISBN: 0-9631212-8-6

No. 10   Alfonso Sastre: ***The Abandoned Doll. Young Billy Tell.*** (*Historia de una muñeca abandonada. El único hijo de William Tell*).
Translated by Carys Evans-Corrales. 1996.
ISBN: 1-888463-00-7

No. 11   Lauro Olmo and Pilar Enciso: ***The Lion Calls a Meeting. The Lion Foiled. The Lion in Love.*** (*Asamblea general. Los leones*)
Translated by Carys Evans-Corrales. 1997.
ISBN: 1-888463-01-5

No. 12   José Luis Alonso de Santos: ***Hostages in the Barrio.*** (*La estanquera de Vallecas*).
Translated by Phyllis Zatlin. 1997.
ISBN: 1-888463-02-3

No. 13   Fermín Cabal: ***Passage.*** (*Travesía*)
Translated by H. Rick Hite. 1998.
ISBN: 1-888463-03-1

No. 14   Antonio Buero-Vallejo: ***The Sleep of Reason*** (*El sueño de la razón*)
Translated by Marion Peter Holt. 1998.
ISBN: 1-888463-04-X

No. 15   Fernando Arrabal: ***The Body-Builder's Book of Love*** (*Breviario de amor de un halterófilo*)
Translated by Lorenzo Mans. 1999.
ISBN: 1-888463-05-8

No. 16   Luis Araújo: ***Vanzetti***
Translated by Mary-Alice Lessing. 1999.
ISBN: 1-888463-08-2

No. 17   Josep M. Benet i Jornet: ***Legacy*** (*Testament*)
Translated by Janet DeCesaris. 2000.
ISBN: 1-888463-09-0

No. 18   Sebastián Junyent: ***Packing up the Past*** (*Hay que deshacer la casa*)
Translated by Ana Mengual. 2000.
ISBN: 1-888463-10-4

No. 19   Paloma Pedrero: ***First Star & The Railing*** (*Una estrella & El pasamanos*)
Translated by H. Rick Hite. 2001.
ISBN: 1-888463-11-2

No. 20   José María Rodríguez Méndez: *Autumn Flower* (*Flor de Otoño*)
Translated by Marion Peter Holt. 2001.
ISBN: 1-888463-12-0

No. 21   Juan Mayorga: *Love Letters to Stalin* (*Cartas de amor a Stalin*)
Translated by María E. Padilla. 2002.
ISBN: 1-888463-13-9

No. 22   Eduardo Galán & Javier Garcimartín: *Inn Discretions* (*La posada del Arenal*)
Translated by Leonardo Mazzara. 2002.
ISBN: 1-888463-14-7

No. 23   Beth Escudé i Gallès: *Killing Time & Keeping in Touch* (*El color del gos quan fuig & La lladre i la Sra Guix*)
Translated by Bethany M. Korp & Janet DeCesaris. 2003.
ISBN: 1-888463-15-5

No. 24   José Sanchis Sinisterra: *The Siege of Leningrad* (*El cerco de Leningrado*)
Translated by Mary-Alice Lessing. 2003.
ISBN: 1-888463-16-3

No. 25   Sergi Belbel: *Blood* (*La sang*)
Translated by Marion Peter Holt. 2004.
ISBN: 1-888463-17-1

No. 26   Cristina Fernández Cubas: *Blood Sisters* (*Hermanas de sangre*)
Translated by Karen Denise Dinicola. 2004.
ISBN: 1-888463-18-X

No. 27   Ignacio del Moral: *Dark Man's Gaze and Other Plays* (*La mirada del hombre oscuro. Papis. Osesnos*)
Translated by Jartu Gallashaw Toles. 2005.
ISBN: 1-888463-19-8

No. 28   Concha Romero: *A Saintly Scent of Amber* (*Un olor a ámbar*)
Translated by Karen Leahy. 2005.
ISBN: 1-888463-20-1 / 978-1-888463-20-0

No. 29   Itziar Pascual: *Gone Astray: Castaways, Holiday Out, Meowless* (*Varadas, Holliday Aut, Miauless*)
Translated by Phyllis Zatlin. 2006.
ISBN: 1-888463-24-4 / 978-1-888463-24-8

ORDER INFORMATION

List price, nos. 2-5, 7-11: $6; nos. 12-29 & rev. 1, 6, $9.
Shipping and handling for one or two volumes, $1.25 each.
Free postage on orders of three or more volumes, within United States.
Special price for complete set of 29 volumes, $135.

Make checks payable to **ESTRENO Plays** and send to:

ESTRENO Plays
c/o Drs. Lamartina-Lens, Berardini   Phone: 1-212-346-1433
Modern Languages Dept.-PNY   E-mail: ilamartinalens@pace.edu
Pace University   sberardini@pace.edu
41 Park Row   Fax: 1-212-346-1435
New York, NY 10038 USA

VISIT OUR WEBSITES:

http://appserv.pace.edu/execute/page.cfm?doc_id=16993
www.rci.rutgers.edu/~estrplay/webpage.html

ESTRENO Plays was founded in 1992 by Martha T. Halsey at Penn State University. In 1998-99 the series moved to Rutgers, The State University of New Jersey, where it was edited by Phyllis Zatlin. Starting in 2005-2006, it has been located at Pace University in Manhattan.

ESTRENO Plays is printed at Ag Press in Manhattan, Kansas.